The Christian Existentialist

The Deems Lectures

The Reverend Charles Force Deems, born in 1820, was deeply concerned with the relationship of science and philosophy to religion. In 1881 he founded the American Institute of Christian Philosophy for the investigation of the most significant questions pertaining to this relationship. In 1895, two years after the death of Dr. Deems, the American Institute of Christian Philosophy endowed a Lectureship of Philosophy at New York University in his honor and for a continuation of the purpose for which the institute had been founded.

Father Häring's lectures were sponsored by the Deems Fund, and were delivered in 1966. Other Deems lectures published by New York University Press are:

Faith and Speculation, by Austin M. Farrar.

The Logic of Religion, by Joseph M. Bochenski, O. P.

THE CHRISTIAN EXISTENTIALIST

*The Philosophy and Theology
of Self-Fulfillment in Modern Society*

Containing the Deems Lectures
delivered at New York University in 1966

by Bernard Häring, C.Ss.R.

NEW YORK: New York University Press
LONDON: University of London Press Limited
1968

© 1968 by New York University
Library of Congress Catalog Card Number 68-13027
Manufactured in The United States of America

Foreword

This book is an expansion of a series of lectures given at New York University in March, 1966. I am deeply grateful to the Committee for the Charles Deems Lectures, especially to Dr. Lee A. Belford, chairman of that Committee and of the Department of Religious Education of New York University. Their invitation, and the lively audience discussions that followed the lectures, provided me the stimulus to put on paper my ideas on personalism and existentialism in Christian ethics.

The book does not claim to present totally new ideas. However, I have used this opportunity to express more fully and precisely a synthesis of the type of personalism that underlies my whole approach to Christian ethics, and to reveal some important implications for ecumenical dialog and the Christian commitment in the secular city.

Personalism and existentialism, as I understand them, integrate essential values of our common Christian and humanitarian tradition, but in their specific forms they reflect the most vital experiences, the hopes and the fears, of mankind in our time. The personalism that confronts the reader here is neither abstract idealistic thinking about person and freedom nor a mere pragmatic response to the burning questions of our pluralistic society. It is, rather, a dispassionate pondering over the shocking events of our age. It tries to discover the hidden fountain of human experience, an understanding of which could strengthen our hopes and guide our energies in relation to the future of man. It is a confrontation with the gigantic tool-makers who think the future of man is entrusted to them alone. It is intended as a challenge and an appeal to modern man to care above all for the wholeness of the human person and the meaningfulness and integrity of interpersonal relationships.

If it is true that we cannot allow ourselves to neglect economic progress, it is even more evident that we must avoid cultural and moral underdevelopment. Man has the power to shape his history. Modern science provides unexpected possibilities to mold the world around us. But for a mankind that wants to be free, the great question is and remains: What are we meant to be as persons before God in our interpersonal relationships, as persons in modern society, as persons who are more than a part of an evolving and changing society and yet cannot be truly ourselves unless we take our individual active roles in it? How can we find our true selves in our effort to shape the future?

I am greatly indebted to my sister, Sr. Lucidia Haering, and to my confrere Father John F. Craghan, for their valuable collaboration. If the English is readable, they deserve the credit for it. I want also to thank Mrs. Ellen MacKenzie for a most careful and competent editing.

Bernard Häring, C.Ss.R.

May 1967
Yale Divinity School
New Haven

Contents

The Christian Existentialist

CHAPTER I

Personalism and Existentialism in Confrontation with Individualism and Collectivism

Among men of all cultures, true human perception and thought is preoccupied with the search for a personalistic understanding of existence. In this essential effort, however, man is, and has been, confronted with endless difficulties. A truly personalistic concept of human existence has been opposed, in turn, by magical philosophies, animism, and even demonism. Equally hostile have been the undue demands for power made by clan, group, and state.

In the modern world, personalism faces three particular enemies: First, the functionary, who dominates almost every area of life; second, a purely technological manner of thinking, an effect peculiar to the epoch of rapid development in the sciences; and third, a philosophy of life that categorizes everything in terms of end and means, cause and effect, and a philosophy of knowledge that treats the person as a mere object, as a thing among things.

I consider personalism and the more humanistic existentialism, first of all, as two aspects of a general vital awareness; forms of the particular spirit of our age with widely divergent characteristics and possibilities for both fulfillment and aberration.

Personalism and existentialism are not synonymous. Their several meanings vary greatly. Nevertheless, a close analysis of personalism and existentialism shows the possibility of a synthesis.

Personalism as a General Vital Awareness

A personalistic vital awareness is a spontaneous and often explosive reaction against a manner of thinking that is *thing*-oriented; against a way of planning and managing that manipulates man solely as an object. Personalism is man's protest against being treated as a cog in a wheel or an object to be exploited.

In our age material civilization has made enormous progress. Man today is more adept than ever before in history in the management of material things. Despite this fact modern man is often disturbed by the increasingly apparent autonomy of industry and its controllers, factors that he himself created. In rebellion against this trend, man is driven to assert his primacy as a person endowed with liberty, as a person with a basic responsibility for his fellowman. He wants to be considered as an individual, not as a functionary in a society composed of boards of directors.

Even before modern man begins to articulate his reaction in precise terms, however, there arises within him a spontaneous vital awareness which communicates itself from man to man. It is an intuitive perception and sensing that first reveals itself in unconscious, and, finally, conscious, reactions. Philosophical and theological reflection, which in some way remains open and attentive to the basic premises of personal existence, attains new impulse and new energy through this awareness of the spirit of the times. It expresses itself in an ardent concern for man, an impartial sharing in the cares, opportunities, and perils of the particular epoch and environment.

In this frame of reference, personalism is a philosophical way of thinking related intimately to the burning questions of our time. It is not disinterested, cold, abstract philosophizing about the essential constitution of personal existence.

It is, rather, a deep concern with the questions of the human person, who revolts the more violently against purely impersonal thought and discussion the more he perceives his own dignity threatened or denied by a society in which he is chiefly an object of administration.

Present-day personalistic thought and awareness must be seen against the background of the innumerable, yet ever-increasing social relationships of a society impregnated by socialized endeavors and undertakings. Here, we are dealing, not with the vital awareness of the hermit, but with the vital awareness and demands of man as confronted with modern medias of communication and methods of influencing and shaping public opinion; in brief, with man totally incapable of existence without these complex social services.

The personalistic concept of life and its corresponding philosophy, which comes to grips with and transforms vital awareness and understanding of the world, permit various forms of personalism. These forms, however, must be carefully distinguished.

It is an impossible undertaking to reduce the different forms of personalism to a basic few. Therefore, I shall merely attempt here to present the decisive forms, together with their predominant phenomena. For this purpose I should like to consider them under three forms, which I call: (1) I-oriented, humanistic personalism; (2) social personalism; and (3) radical I-Thou-We personalism.

The I-oriented Form of Personalism

I-oriented personalism does not refer to the self-worship of the despot, who purposefully reduces all others to the status of means or instruments, nor to the profiteer of both men and objects. It is a personalism that takes every person seriously as an individual; that considers the person essentially as determined by his own need of subsistence and self-perfection. The ethic corresponding to such a personalism concentrates on self-perfection and conceives the essential element of virtue less from a value which calls and invites man than from one's own increase in value.

Greek thought abounds in decisive approaches to this type of personalism. It appears in different forms in Aristotelian eudaemonism and Platonic idealism but is particularly pronounced in the Stoic philosophy of life and ethics, which a certain pantheistic trait prevented from collapsing absolutely into monadism. This type of personalism considers persons essentially as related to one another, at least through the ideas that unite them with the unifying spirit of the world. Yet, the point of reference of each and every person is his lawful concern with self-perfection. In this frame of reference it considers and "uses" everything and everyone.

The emergence of the person is determined chiefly by knowledge; this simultaneously embraces a taking-into-oneself of the other and an actual self-forgetfulness or passing-over-of-oneself. The four cardinal virtues (prudence, fortitude, justice, and temperance) are unquestionably concerned with the harmony of interpersonal relationships, while nevertheless regarded primarily as the harmony within the order of one's own faculties.

An outstanding characteristic of this type of personalism is the place allotted to love. In Stoic thought, love is numbered among the passions to be regarded with suspicion. At a later date, Emmanuel Kant called love "a pathological matter." Christian personalists with a similar philosophy treat love as a theological virtue. For them love is intended to direct the whole *ornatus animae* of the virtues to the supernatural goal, although it is not an essential determinant of the person. According to this philosophy, love is given to man as a commandment with external sanctions of reward and punishment. A specific mark of this mode of thinking is reflected in the concept of love of neighbor. In such a system, the latter is simply an opportunity "to heap up merits" and to prove and increase one's own virtuousness.

This personalism descends easily to a certain individualism. Everyone is his own neighbor. In this frame of reference, man in his sincere concern for self-perfection sees the community and his neighbor as either a help or a hindrance (depending on circumstances). Both community and neighbor fall into the category of means. The complete development of one's individuality is the decisive element, insofar as it entails no conflict with the world. The community must justify itself by serving to develop "my" individuality.

Since the Renaissance this form of personalism has appeared chiefly in the West in a humanism influenced by the culture of antiquity combined with Christian elements. Its influence continues in today's philosophy and theology. Yet it will fail to mirror the ardent life of the spirit of the times if it is not united with new approaches to personalism.

In I-oriented personalism I would include the cultural humanism that, on the one hand, considers man as a goal and not merely as a means and, on the other, is closely connected with a definite form of culture, i.e., the classical or pseudo-classical. It prefers the ancient languages of Latin and Greek to modern languages; speculative learning to the social sciences, to modern empirical psychology, and even to the natural and technical sciences. It exalts theory above practice, contemplation above action.

Nicolai Hartmann, among others, represents a new form of this I-oriented personalism. In his view, man is in dialogue with objective values that are capable of laying claims on him, of ennobling him, and of pronouncing him guilty. Nevertheless, this world of values receives its order from man. Here the human person is opposed to a principle. Hence, it is the affair of the person to construct his own order of values for himself as a "demiurge" and to choose it as his own in absolute self-mastery over principles and values.

The tragedy lies in the fact that the person thereby violates other values. At the same time, this I-oriented value bears proof that the person is higher than all principles.

Social Personalism

The young Karl Marx personified the type of men who, prompted by social fervor, provide approaches to a personal way of thinking but ultimately fail to advance these approaches in their scientific thought. Karl Marx protested vehemently against an inhuman economic system and certain patterns of liberalism that sacrificed human dignity to the brutal mechanism of economic development. In his initial love and turbulence, which recalled that of the Old Testament prophets, Karl Marx was concerned about man. Yet in his subsequent speculative approach, he considered man fundamentally determined by the processes of economics and society.

Insofar as Karl Marx incorporated an ethical prophetism, he demonstrated a certain deep-rooted social personalism, contrary, to be sure, to his scientific system. For him, the end of all socio-economic development was man who had been perfected in absolute brotherliness in the classless society of perfect solidarity; the man unselfishly open for the community. However, the underlying sociological theory intended to direct man's history toward the final goal of a classless society through tensions inherent in the laws of production radically destroys the personalistic approach. According to the Marxist philosophy of history, material development, production, and the social constitution of the economic process determine the ethical, religious, cultural, and political theories of man as well as his practical behavior. Did Marx necessarily expect that the perfect order of *the material components* — of the general economic system — would, in the last phase, produce the perfect man in the classless society? As interpreted by Stalin, Marxism required that individuals as well as whole communities be sacrificed to the inevitable laws of economics.

In opposition to such theory, the ethical socialism of Ferdinand Lasalle and other Christian socialists demands that the order of economics and society be conceived and constructed around the dignity of man. The social structures must be conducive to a fully human existence and the self-development of all men. In contradistinction to Marxism, ethical socialism does not believe in an absolute autonomy of economic development. It calls for the humanization of the economy in all its phases and on all levels.

Modern empirical sociology has demonstrated sufficiently how the individual man and groups of men rely on environmental conditions in their social thought and conduct. Obversely, it also has revealed man's ability to change his environment by cooperative group action. This knowledge has had a lasting influence on both today's systematic and practical theology, particularly in France and Germany.

The moral sermons of the last century were directed to the individual. The person was solely or predominantly addressed in his isolation. Conversion was considered to take place on the I-level. In contradistinction, today's moral and pastoral theory provides a personal and environmental conception. Conversion is a new relationship, not only to God but also to the world at large. Hence, true conversion is lacking if the individual is unwilling to cooperate in creating for himself and others those conditions most favorable to the development of the person in the community. Above all, the religious and social elite are called upon to use their special talents and influence for social improvements. In true justice and love for all, they are to effect the desired and necessary cultural, social, economic, and political renewals and improvements. Every person has a right to a standard of living that will permit him to develop his own personality.

7

Being-a-Person in Word and Love

God's revelation in the person of Jesus Christ gave decisive direction to explicit reflection on the nature of being-a-person in its characteristic openness of self for the Thou. The Bible (particularly the New Testament) makes a unique contribution to our knowledge of a personal mode of existence that is not found in any other philosophy or religion. It is a new understanding of existence, concentrating on a new understanding of person. Today, biblical thought has had a renewed impact on modern personalism. It seems to me, however, that other factors besides biblical renewal have given impetus to this desirable trend. We witness a Christian personalism with a new stamp that in its most profound dimension can match the appeal of the Bible. But its vitality and vigor are derived from the *kairos*, the present moment of salvation. This new personalism has achieved its distinctive features, not merely despite the many dangers threatening genuine personal existence but also in virtue of its experience with these dangers.

The mid-twentieth century has witnessed the horrifying consequences of insane "person-worship." Depersonalized man has been, and is, forced to render this worship to tyrants who, with the aid of modern mass media and mass psychology, exert hypnotizing power over the masses and adroitly organize such worship in the ruthless pursuit of base aims. They either brutally wipe out all resistance against such worship or subject the masses to an extremely efficient brainwashing that is intended to extinguish all personal resistance and expression. It is sufficient in this instance to cite the names of Hitler, Stalin, and Mao Tse-tung.

Add to this startling experience the depersonalizing influences and trends of today's lifestream that pervade all human endeavors, including man's leisure time, in crowded cities.

Even in the best external forms of today's society there are anonymous, cold, and overbearing aspects.

In this momentous hour of history, man values increasingly the intimacy of marriage, the family, friends, and other communities of persons that provide genuine personal contact. In these communities of love he once again feels himself a man in the full sense of the word, i.e., he becomes a person. Consequently, philosophical analysis and reflection take cognizance of these basic experiences of man, while keeping in view the danger that man can be swallowed up by organization.

"What protection is there against the danger of organization? Man once more is faced with the problem of himself. He can cope with every danger except the danger of human nature itself. In the last resort it turns upon man" (Dietrich Bonhoeffer, *Letters and Papers from Prison*. New York: Macmillan, 1965, p. 236).

In his inmost nature, man does not see himself as a manager, nor as one to be managed. Instead, he sees himself as confronted with the thou, whom he loves so tenderly, whom he respects irrespective of purpose or utility, and from whom he receives similar recognition and respect as a person; that is, he receives love.

In Greek and Scholastic-Thomistic tradition, philosophical reflection on being-one's-self took as its chief approach the relation to the "other" by means of rational knowledge. It held that man can have a relation to another (person) and thereby return to his own self. He can return to his own self and be anchored within himself, while he reaches out in thought after that which he himself is not. (In this connection the question arose regarding the Highest Being, the Eternal Thou.) The person realizes his otherness as opposed to all objective things by looking to this double movement: (1) that of opening himself in thought to the universality of being; (2) that of drawing back completely within himself.

In this double movement the constitution of the person is discovered; namely, the substance of an individual nature, which in thought can have a relation with, and yet an aloofness from, another.

I do not intend to deny the justification of this metaphysical view of person. However, it seems to me that the basic reality of person is imperfectly articulated in this view. At any rate, this personalism does not inflame today's philosopher, who reflects on being-a-person in view of the present threat to man from the material world and its organization. The distinction between the efficient, organizational, managerial relationship to things and the speculative, abstract relationship to the "other," to being, does not interest him, at least, not primarily and ardently.

On the contrary, the personal understanding of being-one's-self in confrontation with the Other (with the Thou) possesses the ardent, vivifying breath of the spirit of the times and the intensity of our own basic experience. It is not so much a question of the relationship to being, but of openness for That Who is, the openness *for the Thou*. The most profound experience of man, who feels that he can be and wants to be more than managed organized material, is the encounter with a Thou who takes his I in complete seriousness, i.e., beyond the sphere of organization or means to ends as well as all bare systems of thought.

The special interest of today's personalism is the unprecedented, irreplaceable person in his uniqueness, in his substance, not insofar as he remains alone as a self, but rather as he encounters the Thou and thus finds his own indispensable, unique name.

The self of man in the lonely crowd often experiences the deepest self-estrangement, frustration, and lack of self-communication from which abstract thought and a materially oriented knowledge is totally incapable to free him. Modern psychology recognizes ipsation (from the Latin *ipse*, "self") as a severe illness, a sign of man's immaturity. Ipsation represents man's incapacity for genuine human communication and, in short, his inability to emerge from himself in a genuinely human manner. This illness may indeed remain temporarily submerged while man is totally absorbed in the external activity of work and organization in his conquest of his immediate world. Yet, when he wishes to retire from the material world, such a person is faced with the curse of his incarceration in his own ego, in the loneliness of self.

Man exists as a person in word and in love, i.e., he emerges from himself in such a manner that his remaining-self is not diminished but increased. Love is already implied in the word that is directed to the Other, to the Thou. The deep dialogue that actualizes community between the Thou and the I is more than the mere confrontation, speech, and administration that principally serve organization.

Modern personalism, as represented by such philosophers and theologians as Ferdinand Ebner, Martin Buber, Max Scheler, Emil Mounier, Gabriel Marcel, Theodor Steinbüchel, Romano Guardini, Emil Brunner, Karl Barth, Dietrich Bonhoeffer, Richard Niebuhr, is a personalism of encounter and community in word and love. It is inconceivable that modern personalism can be understood without Christian tradition, although such personalism is intended as an answer to the needs and questions of modern man. For its most vigorous proponents it is more than a mere philosophy. It becomes the expression of religion, of commitment to God in a freely and gratefully accepted commitment to one's fellow-man.

Theological personalism is always three-dimensional, in that it emphasizes the genuine human interpersonal encounter, the initial finding of self in the finding of the Thou, in loving the Other as a person, and in gratefully receiving love from one's neighbor. It stresses this personal existential experience as the basic approach to religion: to God as my true

Thou; before Whom, in the most profound dimensions of my being, I am an "I" — I have a name.

When speaking of this personal approach to religion we must keep in mind the type of world in which we live; that secular world where God as Prime Cause no longer has a place along with and among the many other causalities. God cannot be presented as a means to world mastery. In today's religious experience He is not the great organizer of the material world. For in the area of application of causalities and organizational formation there is present in modern man's experience a fascinating dynamism of one's own ability — and also of one's final peril if there is nothing beyond this world of causalities. (I trust this presentation will not be misunderstood as a contradiction of the Christian dogma of creation.)

The believing personalist does not understand God as a Prime Cause, Who sets up and manages a material world or Who hands it over to be managed. He sees God as the Lover Who is present in word and love, Who, in His desire to have cocelebrants of His love, transcends Himself and invites man to community.

In the beginning there was not a "Prime Cause" Who made things. Rather, "In the beginning was the Word, and the Word was with God, and the Word was God . . . all things were made through Him, and without Him was not anything that was made" (John 1:1-3). This majestic prologue to St. John's gospel does not need demythologizing before the secular world, whereas a philosophy that thinks in categories of causes, means, and ends cannot appeal to the spirit of modern man. On the causal level modern man himself is commanding, so commanding indeed that beyond it he fears for his more profound self.

It was principally Max Scheler who stressed this truth again and again. He stated that pure thought in the categories of causes from which rational man concludes to an Ultimate

Cause does not lead to religion. Religion presupposes that God reveals Himself in word and love, and that man, on his part, is capable of opening himself to this word and this love.

"Objective" thinking (a thinking that makes the other person a mere object among things and principles), to which we attribute the categories of substance and accident — at least according to present-day concepts — does not do justice to the mystery of the person. It cannot explain that profound depth of feeling that takes place in a warm and intimate community of persons. Furthermore, it is particularly unequipped to articulate those final pronouncements of a personalistic religion. A philosophy in which man is regarded basically as a substance determined by certain accidents, no matter how high such "accidental" relationship to God, the Highest Being and Ultimate Cause, may be elevated, nevertheless blocks the way to adoring love.

Within the basic concepts of substance and accidents, good scholastic philosophy, in the last analysis, did not intend to assert that man is first and essentially a substance and then is somehow related to God in a secondary relationship. Nevertheless, the philosophical approach and the dictionary meaning inevitably created the primacy of man's substance (a type of impersonal objectivity). Accordingly, the relationship to God remained, in some way, an external one even though the substance was considered as having been created.

Personalism that is related to vitalized religion essentially emphasizes the truth that *man exists only through the Word*. He is a person by reason of God Who calls and appeals to him. Hence, man's only road to self-realization is that of a total surrender of himself to the call, thereby emerging from himself and advancing to the One to Whom he simply owes himself, because the calling is not something additional to man's reality. The person rather becomes a self precisely through the call. Everything in him and about him is call, response to the call, or a warping of self through an imperfect surrender to the call. Similarly, man's refusal to the call of Him Who has thus summoned him to existence (to-be-with), as well as his sluggishness in listening, grasping, and responding, receive their full significance precisely in view of the Word to which the person owes himself and everything.

The intimate and most profound dimension in man comes to light only in the experience of love. The encounter of the I-Thou is an event in word and love. It is not an "objective" knowing or a teleological investigation — and yet it is a knowing. To be sure, the most real knowing is in love. Knowledge without love remains "objective" (*gegenständlich*), always related to materials and goals. "Objective" knowledge does not penetrate the intimate realm of personal existence. Only love can transcend the limits of the isolated self and reach out to that which exists, to the Thou, and thereby be-with the Thou. As Gabriel Marcel has succinctly phrased it, "to-be is to-be-with." In consequence of the encounter with "the Other" there takes place a genuine insight into self.

A personalism with the orientation that to-be is to-be-with does not imply a dissolution or a disintegration of self. In this context the self and the Thou in the "We" are encountered in true sincerity. But without the relationship to the Thou, without the fundamental appeal from Him Who is simply the fullness of Word and Love, the self would lack all meaning. It could not be present to another and be fulfilled in word and love.

Ultimately, only divine revelation discloses the mystery that God's own love is an ineffable Trinity, a Self in mutual bestowal of word and love. God is an absolute Self in ultimate community, and in this community, which is the Trinity, all true community of persons is rooted.

God summons us to His own Self and chiefly to being-with His love in His Word. At the same time He also calls us to be-with the thou of our fellowman. God's call always confronts us with the thou of our neighbor, open to us in love. Vitalized religion with the living God is a call channeled through one's neighbor that reveals the ultimate dignity, the most profound depth, and the zenith of the human we. "For he who does not love his brother whom he has seen, cannot love God whom he has not seen" (I John 4:20).

The Primacy of Love

The personalism described above does not approach the love of our fellowman within the framework of commandment: "Thou shalt" or "Thou must." Love transcends the material things that can be ordered in the world of organization and management. A commandment-centered outlook admits no access to the real nature of love. In this sense I would mention the personalistic theory so often stated by Max Scheler: "Love cannot be ordered. Love is not a commandment."

Nevertheless, love is *the* New Commandment, that completely new revelation in the moral message of the New Testament. "A new command I give to you, that you love another; even as I have loved you, that you also love one another" (John 13:34). But here the decisive note is that God's love approaches self-centered man in need of redemption, manifesting a deep mystery and a warm reality rather than a bare commandment. This love has been manifested in the person of Jesus Christ. In the Incarnation, love appears as a deeply personal experience, as both the messenger and message of love, as the invitation of joy to love in return and to be-with in love. Redemption flows not from the commandment of love, but is the self-surrendering love itself. Hence, salvation arises only from faith in this love; from the reception of this love in faith. This love inevitably demands a complete readiness to make a radical commitment to itself in all things. The commitment in turn implies a perfect self-surrender to love's rewarding happiness by way of a grateful reciprocating response. Love's very demands are expressions of its sincerity and concern for the beloved. Yet it should be unmistakably clear that even this readiness, so essential for redemption, is not the result of a bare commandment. Rather, it is the fruit of God's benevolent love whereby He reveals Himself to man and thereby draws man's heart and mind to Himself.

In short, salvation comes from faith alone. Faith is hereby understood as that gladdening and liberating "Yes" to the truth that comes to us through Christ and which, in all its aspects, is the saving truth of the love of God.

We may even say that works of justice based in legal justification and egocentric self-perfection are useless, even harmful, to salvation. However, this does not refer to the works of justice in the biblical sense, nor to the correctly understood perfection of man. We do not refer here to the good works that express a fundamental openness to the Thou and the We and already bear the beginning marks of faith. Our reference is only to a work-articulated justification that bears witness to a covert or overt worship of man's ego.

However, it holds true for both faith and love (experienced in faith): that they do not lack the fruits of the Spirit. "But the fruit of the Spirit is love, joy, peace, patience, kindness, goodness, faithfulness, gentleness, self-control; against such there is no law" (Gal. 5:22–23). Faith in the living God is filled with love and acts in love.

The primacy of love over the *commandment* of love and hence over all commandments — which, in the final analysis, merely translate and mediate love itself and its commandment into actual life situations — becomes especially clear in the fifteenth chapter of St. John's gospel. Our Lord began by announcing the great mystery and deep abyss of His love and that of the Father. This indicates clearly that the foundation and beginning of salvation is not commandment — be it the most beautiful of all commandments — but love. "Love one another as I have loved you" (John 15:12). It is to-be-with in the love of Christ, which is received as a gift. Therefore, man receives the impelling invitation filled with personal responsibility for salvation: "As the Father has loved me, so have I loved you; abide in my love" (John 15:9). To-be-with or to abide in love invites the creature to a community of love with Christ in His self-giving love. Man becomes humble. He frees himself from the fetters that incarcerate him in his own ego. He comes to experience his true self, his true name, and the fulfillment of Our Lord's promise: "If you abide in me, and my words abide in you, ask whatever you will, and it shall be done for you" (John 15:7). This "whatever you will" must be understood in context. Ultimately it means: whatever this to-be-with in love wills.

To-be-with in love — with Him Who is the full revelation of love — must find its true expression in a new relationship to our fellowman. This being-with is dynamic; it has the power to renew all interpersonal relationships. "He who abides in me, and I in him, he it is that bears much fruit" (John 15:5). To-be-with in love cannot be translated into a bare "Thou shalt," but manifests itself in the joy that accompanies each new knowledge and experience of this love. "These things I have spoken to you, that my joy may be in you, and that your joy may be full" (John 15:11).

All this explains how Our Lord proclaims love for our fellowman as a *commandment*. It is the personal appeal, the loving exhortation of Him Who is Love and at the same time lavishly bestows it. Hence, the commandment is a modality, a form, a joyful articulation of love itself.

Love cannot reduce the beloved to a condition of slavery.

Love renders man's obligation a free offering and points the way to a totally new commitment to love's demands. In the same connection, Our Lord said to His disciples: "No longer do I call you servants, for the servant does not know what his master is doing; but I have called you friends, for all that I have heard from the Father I have disclosed to you" (John 15:15).

Whoever understands the full implications of community in love will also realize that the living personal appeal of love is infinitely more powerful than any mere commandment that either does not proceed from love or fails to contain love or cannot be fully understood in the context of love.

Thus, when we say that the Christian is not under commandments and law but under the mild power of grace, of self-surrendering love (cf. Rom. 6:14), we do not undermine but rather point to the full dynamism of the moral life. The Christian personalist may ask with St. Paul: "Do we then overthrow the law by this law of faith? By no means! On the contrary, we are placing morality itself on a firmer footing" (Rom. 3:31). It is important to remember that, according to our understanding, the word "law" or the word "commandment" enjoys an infinitely higher value and richness of meaning. It is the presence of the power of love. The law of grace, the law of faith, is totally new.

Love Is Not a Superstructure

Love is not something added extrinsically to being-a-person. Nothing would be further from the truth than the attempt to understand the person chiefly as an individual subsistent nature in which rationality and subsistence would be the whole foundation and to regard love as a form of superstructure imposed on the person. Of course, at one time or another we have met highly intellectual and self-sufficient individuals who, despite their undeniable administrative and creative abilities, nevertheless were incapable of genuine human love and affection; who even did not expect love from others. Yet, the question remains: Do they truly live on the level of human persons? Have they ever discovered their real self, their true human nature?

Love is the person's great potential because it originates from the appealing Word that breathes forth love. Man's own nature and the very nature and meaning of love are lost when man is incapable of genuine reciprocating charity toward others.

Biblical anthropology is a part of the doctrine of redemption. In turn, the doctrine of redemption belongs to the correct conception of man. Thus, we might summarize: inordinate self-seeking destroys and perverts love and self, while a genuine giving of self in humble service to others brings man to his fullest self-realization. This is the message of the Paschal mystery. Christ did not seek His own honor and glory, nor His own will: "He did not consider Himself" (Rom. 15:3). He came forth from the Father and He returned to the Father. He dedicated Himself to the Father in the service of His brothers. Therefore, the Father exalted Him and gave Him a name that is above all names. The Paschal mystery unfolds the basic constitution of personal existence.

From the very beginning, the plan of God's creative love is to create man to His own image and likeness. Man has estranged himself from God by yielding to the temptation of drawing his being-a-person, his wisdom, his freedom, his life from his own self. Yet, the inconceivable grandeur of man's personal existence reveals its fullest magnificence only in the love manifested in Christ, his way and his life.

It is not my intention to explore in depth the question of how this view preserves and explains the traditional doctrine on the unmerited gift of the supernatural. It is sufficient to say that our personalism can establish the gratuitousness of redemption more profoundly than can a description of a *natura pura*, a purely natural being-a-person, in which the hearkening to the word coming from God as well as the experience of love do not appear to be the basic components. We are not interested here in what kind of men God could have created. Our outlook is directed to historical man in the profound dimensions of his estrangement from God and His invitation to intimate fellowship with Him. Thus we can see that the essential constitution of the person in word-response and love can actually manifest itself, to a greater or lesser degree, beyond the limits of the visible Church, even beyond the limits of Christianity itself. However, we never sever this reality from the living God of real history, for in all these things we give glory to God, the Father of our Lord Jesus Christ.

A philosophical ethics in which love does not represent the loftiest and truest possibility of man has not yet probed the innermost depth of man's being.

In this regard, the ethics of Confucianism, in which goodness is the first of the basic virtues, is much closer to the Christian concept of man than is the traditional system of virtues (prudence, fortitude, justice, and temperance), where love is added on the supernatural plateau as something extrinsic to man's "natural" basic virtues. Of course, no theologian maintains that the reception of a love such as Christ has revealed to us belongs merely to the concept of man as man. The historical man in all the fibers of his being is created and fashioned for Him.

That system of philosophy, in which love for God and neighbor is an addition or an external law referring to a different plane of existence, is a philosophy of unredeemed man and is itself unredeemed. It merely tends to lock man more securely within his own egoistic self.

The Being-One's-Own of Each Person

The personalism that tends to an ethics of self-perfection starts by analyzing the being-one's-self of the individual nature. Attention is focused chiefly on individuality, which is more or less consciously equated with being-a-person. Individuality actually exists only in the personal order; each person exists only in individual uniqueness.

The personalism that looks principally to the fellowship of persons in word and love by no means ignores individuality; for its philosophical approach is directed to a perverted managerial humanity that could degrade the individual to the level of a mere functionary. The mutual confrontation of the Thou and the I becomes so profoundly stirring, rewarding, and enriching because persons encounter themselves in absolute uniqueness. The thou of our neighbor is not exchangeable, although every man can become our neighbor, our immediate thou. He becomes our thou precisely in his own unique, inimitable person with all his potentialities and needs, with his inexpressible name, and faced with God Who calls him to unrepeated uniqueness in openness to the Thou and We.

The personalism found in an ethics of self-perfection all too easily descends to individualism, i.e., the individual becomes the constant point of reference.

Our personalism of fellowship in word and love does take individuality in all seriousness. This is implied in every statement. But it becomes clear that its complete and genuine brilliance is reflected only when it places itself at the service of the thou and of the community and from that vantage point grasps all its true potentialities.

Existentialism

Existentialism can combine an individualistic personalism as well as a personalism of fellowship in love. Its distinguishing mark, which is peculiar to the vital awareness of modern man, always seems to be the violent rejection of all that is stereotyped and uniform in a traditionalism that lacks vitality and runs counter to the spirit of the times. The existentialist stresses the originality of his each particular decision in opposition to the impersonal "they" who let themselves be carried along by the tide of popular opinion. He wishes to direct his own existence. He wants to show himself and others that he is literally *himself*.

Modern existentialism possesses many forms. There is an essential difference between the schools of Martin Heidegger and Karl Jaspers, on the one hand, and those of Jean-Paul Sartre and Simone de Beauvoir, on the other. However, they all share an ardent concern for individuality, for the individual in his spontaneity, in his primary proper responsibility for himself. Their philosophical approach aims at man's stepping out of an anonymous existence and emerging from himself in true being-one's-own. But this emergence is considered chiefly in view of man cast away to the outskirts of personal existence and imperiled by forces crushing his true self.

Existentialism can combine a one-sided occasionalism that out of a pure and simple concern for the spontaneity and originality of each decision — of each self-emergence — forgets the continuity of self. Protest against stereotyped orderliness thus descends to disorderliness, that is, a discontinuity resulting from arbitrariness.

We are interested in uniting harmoniously the spontaneity of what is original with attentiveness to what currently is new, to what is unique in each situation, with a view to man in his imperishable being-one's-own and being-one's-self. Man in his being-one's-own and being-one's-self is the absolute condition for the encounter of the thou and the I and for the meaningfulness of community, for the significance of the we.

Genuine personalism as well as the best type of existentialism both esteem liberty; in fact, they bear the mark of an ardent concern for the liberty of each person. Personalism of the being-with, of the fellowship of the thou and the I in the community of the we, must pay the greatest attention to the study of true, personal and community creative freedom and to the responsibility of the self for himself when confronted by the thou. It is evident, however, that the existentialism that takes up the cause of freedom without paying full attention to the basic forms of dialogue, of love, and of community in truth and genuine charity, can lead only to arbitrariness, chaos, and even to the destruction of the community.

The Person as Seen in His Totality

The various currents of personalism reach their point of division through their distinctive view of man's bodily components. Again and again personalism has sought to counteract certain spiritualizing tendencies. Under the guise of defending the person's dignity as spirit, they either cast suspicion on the body, regarding it as an adversary of personal existence, or else fail to integrate man's bodily components into their theories.

Man as a person has body-soul totality. Not only the spirit is personal; the spiritual soul of the human person, by its very nature, is most intimately related to the body. Man completely possesses the word in perception and communication only when his body is engaged. The animated body is itself "word"-communication; it is the visage turned to the thou. It is communicative; it is the manifestation of love. Man's hands are not intended only for grasping things in instrumental fashion; they are meant also to be offered to others in reciprocating handshake.

Unquestionably, man's body is threatened constantly by a certain danger of the unspiritual, the impersonal. Yet, this danger does not proceed only from man's body. It is rooted in the person's innermost way of seeking the self, insofar as the whole person isolates himself or is activated by purely utilitarian motives. The more the whole personality bears the stamp of loving communication, the more the body also reveals its "personalizing" dignity. It becomes increasingly a visible communication, a fervent openness to love in profound composure.

In his relation to the thou and to the world, the human person stands in need of his emotions, which are not intended to throw the spirit into confusion but to be marked by the word of love. Without the emotions, the human spirit is powerless, as if deprived of life. However, the emotions without the control of the spirit are unruly and depersonalized.

The meaning of a personalistic view of the body becomes especially evident in the moral teaching on marriage. A purely instrumental concept of marriage cannot comprehend the meaningfulness of the marriage act when here and now it is not intended as a means to the end of procreation. The alternatives are viewed as either a procreative act or a selfish quest of pleasure. Such an outlook ignores the marriage act as mutual self-realization, as an *incorporated* word, a communication, in which the partners mutually reveal their most intimate self and their true conception of their covenant of love, their communion in word and love. In the latter context, higher moral demands are made on the spouses without producing frustrations. It is a question of the ennobling demands of a love in perpetual quest of greater openness for the thou, a love that looks for a more meaningful communication. Such a love as this, which in word-message-appeal-response, in complete bodily dedication, and in indissoluble being-with in the community of life as a whole, has the property of opening itself to the Third Person in the covenant of love, to God Who is absolutely the Faithful One, God in His creative love. This love precludes all unworthy egoism in either partner. Like God's overflowing love, it desires the cocelebrants of this particular love, it seeks children. Not every marital union is a procreative act, but every marriage union in true self-surrender refecundates mutual love and increases harmony and joy, and thereby provides the ideal preparation for the vocation of parenthood.

An unsuspected sublime dimension of the personalistic notion of the body comes to light in a consideration of the *Word of God made Man*. We could even go so far as to say: in a consideration of the Word of God made Body. "And the Word became flesh and had presence amongst us" (John 1:14). Christ now continues the eternal dialogue of love with the Father in His body. Obviously we refer here to the animated, personalizing body. The prayer of Christ, which continued to His last dying breath on the Cross, is this: "A body hast Thou prepared for me; . . . I have come to do Thy will" (Heb. 10:5-7).

The body that sacrificed itself and the soul that delivered itself into the hands of the Father are the greatest accomplishment of the Word on earth. We are here confronted with the final, most perfect expression of the Word as message and response of love to the Father in the eloquent, loving fellowship with all men. Easter is proof that final glorification is also a glorification of the body.

A Personalistic View of History

One form of existentialism, concerned chiefly with the self-assertion of its original liberty, does not know how to study man's history adequately. However, the opposite holds true of that personalism that takes its orientation from the entrance of God's Incarnate Son into history. The history of the world — man's world — finds its basic composition, its true ring, and its complete harmony only in that Word which, not only creates everything, but brings it to perfection and completion.

The human person has a history, for man can perceive the Creator's call in his very self, in the Creator's gifts to him, and in the world around him. He can reply or refuse to reply. The world is a history of refusal by self-centered men to heed the word of God, but ultimately a history of acceptance, a history whose true meaning is revealed in the Word of God. The individual man has a history and is history. He is conditioned by history and he can shape history. This important truth should be seen from the aspect of Word, which is message, appeal, and response. Man enrols himself in the liberating course of history, which attains its perfection in the Word of God only on condition that he take seriously the "word," the appealing message of history coming to him and codetermining him, that he seek to grasp its significance, and that he attempt to respond to it in the best possible manner.

Christ is a new beginning, a new chord, a new message in human history. He is the turning point of history, but not in a historyless sense. He fully submits Himself to history, He takes it over, He bears its mark in both His body and soul, and thus gives it a new meaning of adoring and liberating love. He permeates and animates everything, even suffering, but particularly that suffering which, permeated by love, is fully directed to the thou of each individual and the we of all.

The Word made Flesh shows man that everything, even the limitations of his own ego, can become steppingstones to true self-hood open to the Thou of God and neighbor.

Passionate Love for the Universe

One of the great merits of Teilhard de Chardin is that he understood how to combine a predominantly scientific ethos, devoted to examining the actual, with a personalistic vision of the universe. The personalistic conception of the universe is not new. For the Christian it is part of the doctrine of creation and redemption. It has found its classical expression in chapter eight of Paul's Epistle to the Romans. Man who has been set free in his jubilant acceptance of the law of the Spirit in Christ Jesus (cf. Rom. 8:2) feels an impelling appeal in his purified relationship to the Creator and Redeemer. It is the appeal of the whole created world to be incorporated in the realm of His liberating love, since it is already incorporated into this realm by the Creator and Redeemer.

Today's personalism, at the very outset, often tempts man to flee from the public sphere; above all, from the sphere of modern economy into the intimate community of persons and to attach only minimal importance to conditions of the economic life. Such a position cannot overcome the danger to the person from the "functionary." If a personalistic approach is to influence life, the whole area of man's existence must be transformed in the perspective of personalism, of "word" and love — but always in the proper proportion and at the proper level of communication. The constitution of Ecumenical Council Vatican II, relating to the Church in the World of this Time, is an important contribution to a personalistic view of shaping the world that indeed does justice to the brotherhood of men. Its conception of work in the modern economic life may serve as an example.

> Human activity, to be sure, takes its significance from its relationship to man. Just as it proceeds from man, so it is ordered toward man. For when a man works he not only alters things and society, he develops himself as well. He learns much, he cultivates his resources, he goes outside of himself and beyond himself. Rightly understood, this kind of growth is of greater value than any external riches which can be garnered. A man is more precious for what he is than for what he has. Similarly, all that men do to obtain greater social justice, wider brotherhood, a more human ordering of social relationships has greater worth than technical advances (art. 35).
> Human labor which is expended in the production and exchange of goods or in the performance of

economic services is superior to the other elements of
economic life . . . This labor comes immediately from
the person who, so to speak, not only gives the things
of nature his own imprint, but at the same time
subdues them to his will. Under ordinary circumstances,
labor is the means whereby a man supports himself
and his family, is joined to his fellow men and serves
them, and can exercise genuine charity and be a partner
in the work of bringing divine creation to perfection
(art. 67).

However, man cannot maintain this personalistic attitude
in his economic productivity, if in his confrontation with the
created world he assumes an attitude of utilitarian productivity. In the question of world conquest, man really remains
an image of God only if he is able to gaze in wonderment at
God's work as manifested in creation; when he still continues
to adore God. The man who worships is able to uncover
from the world of created things the message: "The heavens
are telling the glory of God" (Ps. 18:1). He sees in all created things the generous love of the common Creator and
Father. For such a man all things are an invitation to honor
God in response and responsibility, while he humanizes the
sphere of material things by paying attention to interpersonal
relations in all his undertakings. Hence, it is obviously legit-
imate to distinguish the sphere of material things with its objectivity and appropriateness from the immediate sphere of
persons. However, religion does not allow any conduct that
runs counter to the meaning of things in their fundamental
relatedness to the person; it likewise forbids every false per-
sonification of things.

Degrees of Personal Outlook

To apply personalistic statements taken from the most intimate encounter of persons to all social relationships and

even to their relation to material things without distinction would be a modern, revised version of animism. The assurances of love of engaged people do not fall within the same category as a bank transaction for a loan. But even in the latter case it is a question of dealing with persons. A friendly "hello," attention to what the others are saying, a sincere "thank you" to an official or a salesclerk — all belong to a personalistic conception of existence. There is obvious danger of a split personality (schizophrenia) if genuine communication, warmheartedness, and sincere affection were to be limited to the confines of family life and personal acquaintances, while a cold and impersonal atmosphere prevailed in business and social circles.

Animism profoundly degraded the dignity of the person, while endowing plants, animals, even stones with the same or similar qualities as men. Extreme spiritualism devitalized the body, causing the whole universe to look on, speechless. The true personalistic solution lies in the golden mean. Everything must be understood from the aspect of "Word" and love. Everything is created in the Word, but not everything is capable of understanding the Word (appealing message) and transmitting it as complete word (response and message in love). All creatures are made for God's honor, but man is still, in a wholly unique manner, God's adorer and eulogizer.

Primitive countries, the modern great powers, or even the future world union of nations are quite different from the patriarchal family unit or the clan. The transference of intimate familial address, of the closely knit family structure, to the more impersonal relationships of men in modern societies is opposed diametrically to man's social nature and proves detrimental to both the understanding of the intimate community and the proper structures of public relations. Modern ways of living do not necessarily jeopardize our sphere of personal existence. Love can and must pervade all spheres of human endeavors and guide man in his dealings with others;

but it must adopt that wavelength that is attuned to the intimate community or to life in society and organization.

In ethics, love is of prime importance. Yet, this love must find its appropriate modes of expressions in all areas of human existence and in full articulation of the person in all his dimensions. Part of this truth is formulated in the traditional teaching on the virtues: love, although paramount, does not render prudence, fortitude, justice, temperance, and the other virtues useless; on the contrary, it is in these virtues that love finds its full vitality, its variety of expression, and its true relationship. Love does what truth demands. Yet, truth is infinitely rich and demands, therefore, an ever new effort.

CHAPTER II

Religion and Morality;
Fellowship and Responsibility

The question of the essence of religion must be distinguished from the question of how individual men of various cultures approach religion. Both questions, however, are of interest to us here. This particular avenue of approach implies special advantages, but also specific dangers. If the man of our modern society is religious at all, how does he experience religion? And how can one best explain to him what religion in general, but especially what the Christian religion, is?

A glance at the psalms or at similar documents embodying man's search for identity shows us how men who lived from the fruits of the earth understood religion and how they related it to their daily experiences. For many nations in the historical environment of Israel, Mother Earth was the foremost deity. Gods who determined the weather were associated with her presence.

The religion of the chosen people of the Old Testament was very different. For the Israelite there was only one God — the God of the Covenant. Yet, in the Israelite's religious thought and in his prayers the promised land "flowing with milk and honey" remained the ultimate goal. Fidelity or infidelity to the God of the Covenant was reflected in fruitful and barren years, in the rain that revived the parched earth or the heavy, leaden sky that withheld the blessing of a rich harvest.

In the life of a pastoral and agricultural society, solidarity was held as a religious concept. The nomadic tribes usually formed patriarchal family groups who migrated as a unit from famine-stricken or stormswept areas to find a new home blessed by God's graciousness. In a sedentary agricultural society, the concept of solidarity encompassed a whole people. When they were visited by plagues of locusts, mice, and other vermin, the people united against a common scapegoat, usually a single "evildoer," whom they held responsible for the gods' anger. A notable example of solidarity within a more specialized group was the casting overboard of Jonah by the crew of a ship imperiled by storm. In each case, the solidarity was achieved against a force beyond the control of the unit and created a spiritual bond between its members.

This background is an aid in understanding the work of the prophets in Israel. The prophets shared the basic experiences of a pastoral and agricultural society with the people of that society. But they possessed a deeper personal religious insight that permitted them to resist the danger of identifying religion with everyday experiences. They gave a deeper meaning to the psychological-social point of departure and showed the possibilities of advancing beyond it to spiritual union with God. Nevertheless, their work constantly revolved about the living man and his special modes of experience.

The prophet Ezechiel could set forth the totally personal responsibility of each individual, his immutable self before God, so powerfully and so effectively, because the historical context admitted of a particular openness for this interpretation. The Israelites were scattered among the nations. The basic truth of the covenant would have been dangerously obscured if in this new situation the group-responsibility had been presented as simply that of a tribe of shepherds or a small cluster of farmers. Ezechiel showed how each individual stood before God with his own dispositions and his own deeds (cf. Ezechiel 18 ff.).

A terrifying historical experience, a radical change in the environment and in the economic structure did not destroy the religion of the people of Israel. Instead, it allowed them to achieve totally new accents, new ways of religious experience. Religion was intensified; it became personal, without losing sight of the claims of the community.

Our question is, therefore: what avenue of approach to religion, particularly to the religion revealed in Christ, does our new world favor? If we want to speak to this world in a credible manner about the living God, we must take into account the thought and reaction patterns of today's man. This requires that we liberate ourselves from the images, parables, and experiments that awakened religious response in the past, but which are foreign to the life and experience of man today.

There have been attempts in our century to invent new religions — or, better, substitute religions — that are direct, quasi-religious exaltations of the experiences of mass organization and power. Here belongs the religion of blood and race utilized in Nazism: the cult of the masses, the organized worship of the ruthless organization. Marxism, to a great extent, belongs in this category. One ultimately expects an earthly paradise from the iron laws of production processes as well as from the essential elements of exploitation and class hatred used to lead to the final liberation of the worker class. The "believers," who let themselves be managed and dispatched by the apparatus of the communist state, are promised that by so doing they contribute to the final redemption of humanity. Absolute faith in technical progress is to include faith in man, to exclude any faith in a God Who is Love in Person.

Besides these myths of the twentieth century, which are a weak superstructure of the organized and managed society, there is an empirical approach to true religion that corresponds to the innermost depths of man: his love that is open to the Thou. The segment of humanity that has learned to create a truly personal life while pursuing the economic life and the controlled leisure time of its society, is especially close to the essentials of true religion: *community with God in word and love.*

Christ, the Prototype of Religion

In his *Dialogue with Trypho the Jew*, Justin, one of the most influential Christian thinkers of the second century, repeatedly calls Christ the covenant (chaps. 11, 24, 43, 51, 65). In so doing he means to emphasize as explicitly as possible the essence of the Christian religion as opposed to the legalistic religion of the Pharisees.

In the person of Christ the divine and the human confront each other in the most intimate union. He is the personal revelation of the love of the Father. His purpose in coming was to render visible to man the length and the breadth, the height and the depth, of the mystery of divine love through His life and death and His humanity. He is, however, not only messenger and message from God. He is at the same time the most complete reply of love to God. In Him it is apparent that the man who is united with the Father in heaven can lead his fellowmen to God through a fervent, powerful, and selfless love. In Christ's reply to the Father all men are included.

Religion as Faith and Community of Faith

God's revelation of Himself in His Word calls man to faith. Confronted by God's revelation, man experiences the knowledge that his own salvation, his true self and the fulfillment of his loftiest possibilities depend on faith. What, then, is faith in the sense of personal religion?

It is more than the bare acknowledgment that God exists.

Pure abstract thought about God and intellectual acceptance of religious truths can remain imbedded in "objective" categories, so that one fails to reach the living God. Only a factual, objective distance, not a community, is created.

Faith is not a mere whim or fancy. Faith does not emerge from man's own subconscious or depth perception, although it appeals to these levels of man's nature and brings them into accord with the whole man. Faith presupposes that the personal God makes Himself known to man and throws open the heart, will, and intellect of man to community with Him. In the Christian understanding, faith is based on God's own word and work.

"Through the revelation, the invisible God out of the abundance of His love speaks to men as friends and lives among them, so that He may invite and take them into fellowship with Himself" (Ecumenical Council Vatican II's Constitution on Divine Revelation, art. 2).

Creation itself is revelation: for it is created in the Word and hence signifies a word addressed to man, who is created in God's image and likeness and is capable of hearing and replying.

"God, who through the Word creates all things and keeps them in existence, gives men an enduring witness to Himself in created realities" (*ibid.*, art. 3).

God makes Himself known to man in manifold ways, chiefly through men and women who are on fire with the spirit of piety and love. His final, everlasting, and conclusive Word is His Incarnate Son. "He sent His Son, the eternal Word, who enlightens all men, so that he might dwell among men and tell them of the innermost being of God" (*ibid.*, art. 4).

Salvific faith, through which religion becomes life, is the grateful, joyful acceptance of the living Word of God and a trusting self-commitment of man's whole intellect, heart, and will. Faith is the reply from the depths of the person, looking to the Person, Who is messenger and message. Faith is the fundamental event between the Thou of God and the I of man. Through it, man becomes an "I-self," because he is addressed by God as thou. In faith man emerges from himself and enters into the most intimate community with God. In faith man becomes verbal in the most complete sense: he expresses his most profound being before God and to God. In Christ, God does not reveal mere things or abstract truths; He reveals Himself and His Will to beatific community. In faith man says "yes" not only to God's truth as truth, but to saving truth: he answers "yes" to his belonging to God in love.

Community of Faith

In Alfred Rosenberg's *Myth of the Twentieth Century* the follower of the Nazi philosophy of life becomes a unit of the mass. He lets himself be moved and carried along. He becomes impersonal, even to the extent that he takes part in the most horrible crimes against humanity without thinking of his own guilt.

In the event of Christian faith — as well as in every religious event of faith that has the same basic structure — the person is summoned in a unique fashion to himself. He reveals himself in word; he finds himself in the love that he receives and to which he responds. Faith is the opposite of a mere presence in the mass. However, it is not individualistic. The personal appropriation of faith cannot hide the fact that the community of believers is involved in transmitting and driving home the Good News, and that living faith leads to a community of faith.

The decisive role of the community is brought out uniquely in the high priestly prayer of Jesus: the becoming-one of His disciples, who witness to the world that faith establishes genuine community, is to awaken faith in the revelation ". . . that they may all be one; even as thou, Father, art in me, and I in thee, that they also may be in us, so that the world may believe that thou hast sent me" (John 17:20–21).

The more believing the community, the more it is a community in word and love, the more will the individual be addressed in a fully personal way. It also holds true that the more believing the individual, and the more fully he opens himself personally to God's salvific truth and surrenders himself in faith to God, the more will his attitude of faith lead him to the community. In revealing Himself God addresses each individual, but He calls him in community and to community.

Christ reveals Himself in a totally personal way to the individual person: to Peter, to John, to Philip. But His word and His person establish at the same time a community of disciples. His own get to know Him more and more. His word, His love, and His person gather them and call them together.

Faith in Jesus incorporates the highest freedom of personal decision in the community of disciples. Each one is called to himself. He must decide for himself. If he refuses faith, then the Master Himself challenges him: "Will you also leave Me?" The element of freedom alone is truth and love with which this truth confronts man.

Worship of God and Salvation of Man

The decision in favor of personalistic religion takes place in worship. For the true worshiper God is more than a pure means for his own salvation. Worship is the fullest "yes" to God's majesty and dignity, but by its very nature it includes the belief that God intends to enter into community with man. In worshiping God both elements are expressed: reverence and love, loving fear and fearful love in a "harmony of contrasts" that is, to be sure, always exposed to dangers (cf. Rudolf Otto's well-known book *Das Heilige*).

Worship is the highest expression of the fact that the religious man takes God in absolute earnestness. He glorifies Him, he praises Him, he thanks Him. Another experience inextricably bound up with worship is that of one's absolute dependence on God, which through trust in the God of Revelation becomes a saving experience. "God is my salvation, my Redeemer and Helper; in Him alone do I find my fulfillment."

In its pure and truly personal form the prayer of petition is a trusting and humble acknowledgment of one's total dependence on God. It is a glorification of the fact that God wishes to be man's salvation. Nevertheless, the prayer of petition can become opposed to worship and a personal relationship to God when one's glance is focused not, on God primarily, but on one's own material needs. This danger consists especially in a piety that stems chiefly from the experience of dependence on God for a rich harvest and other bounties.

Temporal gifts play an important part in the piety depicted in the psalms. But that does not mean that God thus becomes a mere means for temporal prosperity. Rather, the truly pious man values these things more as a sign and a word which assures him of God's favor than as a means of pure utility.

Catholic sacramental devotion of the past centuries discloses a certain tension between the spirit of worship and the tendency to tie in one's own quest for "salvific goods" with worship or to accentuate salvation and "salvific goods." Sound theology and deep devotion always have emphasized the personal aspect of the spirit of worship, even in grateful acceptance. Vatican Council II's Constitution on the Liturgy is clear testimony to the dialogued personal understanding.

> The sacred liturgy is above all things worship of the divine majesty; it likewise contains much instruction for the faithful. For in the liturgy God speaks to His

people and Christ is still proclaiming the Gospel. And the people reply to God both by song and prayer (art. 33).

The relationship between adoration and personal-social salvation becomes most apparent in Sacred Scripture, especially where it treats of the revelation of God's name, God's glory, and God's holiness.

The two great themes of religion and true worship are God's Self-Revelation and God's plan of salvation. God glorifies His name through the salvation He brings to His people. He seems to subordinate His glory to His design of salvation, but, in revealing His name, God stresses His supreme and transcendent dignity. Furthermore, the context of the divine communication reveals another fact with even greater clarity: In His name God reveals Himself to us as the Lord of the whole of history, which He makes into a history of salvation for His adorers. That Israel must adore Him and invoke His name is a sign of His salvific will: "God also said to Moses, 'Say this to the people of Israel. The Lord the God of your fathers, the God of Abraham, the God of Isaac, and the God of Jacob, has sent me to you: this is my name forever, and thus I am to be remembered throughout all generations' " (Exod. 3:15).

The name of Yahweh does not convey to the people of Israel a conceptual or abstract notion of self-existent being, though God is indeed all that; but rather the image of God Who is the mighty helper in deeds, Who chooses to be close to His people with His protection. He is the Lord God, the Holy One, Who says: "I am the Lord your God, who brought you out of the land of Egypt, out of the house of bondage" (Exod. 20:2). Thus, the name of God denotes His dignity and becomes through divine condescension the leitmotif of our salvation. God manifested His name to His people for no reason but His love. His people must give glory to His name in loving adoration and in absolute trust in Him. Then they will see that God is their Saviour.

The Book of Isaias in all its parts bears the profound impress of the threefold "holy" that the cherubim utter before the throne in adoration. God is the Holy One of Israel. But this expression of the *myserium tremendum* also connotes the *mysterium fascinosum* of our salvation. "I will help you, says the Lord; your Redeemer is the Holy One of Israel" (Isa. 41:14). God the All-Holy manifests His holiness and thus sanctifies a people as His own.

The revelation of the glory of God is both awesome and beatifying. It brings man to an increasing awareness of his sinfulness, but it also makes him exult in being allowed to adore God, his Saviour. God lives in the midst of His people through His glory; He shelters them and lends ear to their petitions, so that they may be finally permitted to behold His glory in all its fullness (cf. Isa. 66:10 ff.). God glorifies Himself in bringing salvation to men. But precisely because of this fact, man must seek his salvation in the loving adoration and glorification of God.

Only in the measure in which we know and love the name of God can we hope for the fullness of salvation: a sharing in the blissful covenant proffered to us by God's loving mercy. Only in the measure in which we adore the all-holy God do we thus respond to the revelation of the glory of God by dedicating our entire existence to His glory.

All of God's Self-Revelation in the Old and New testaments has its goal in the beatifying realization that "God is love." God manifests His supreme glory as loving majesty. He glorifies Himself by drawing us to His tender embrace with the ineffable power of His love.

Cultic Community and Salvific Community

The revelation of God's name and majesty unites men in the worship and love of God. Groups of men, and ultimately the whole of humanity, do not attain true unity without the spirit of worship. The book of Genesis shows this in the case

of Adam and Eve, who are the representatives and proto-
types of those who pursue their salvation and freedom by re-
fusing to worship. Immediately after the sin, which is basically described as a refusal to worship, Adam and Eve accuse
each other (Gen. 3:12). The consequences of the sin are
fratricide (Gen. 4:8), polygamy (disdain for women), bru-
tality, and vindictiveness (Gen. 4:23–24).

Saint Paul's Epistle to the Romans takes up this theme
anew. One of Paul's major tenets is that the refusal to worship brings all "unsalvationness" into the world and "unsalvationness," in turn, brings every type of perversion (cf. Rom.
1:18–32). Karl Marx asserted that religion as such alienates
man from himself or, more precisely, discloses his self-
alienation, which is rooted in an inverted economic order. On
the contrary, a true understanding of religion makes it quite
clear that from its very nature it not only unites men in worshiping the same Lord and Father but also reflects the abundance of salvation in the very brotherhood of men. In his unrelenting critique Karl Marx never envisioned true religion.

Vatican Council II, notably in the Constitution on the
Church in the Modern World, has taken into account the
fact that the phenomenon of irreligiousness and atheism results in part from unsuitable forms of religious expression by
religions. External worship of God — if it does not unite
men in that worship — and the quest of salvation in God —
when it is intimately linked with hardness of heart and in-
justice against one's fellowmen — cannot be genuine and
hence cannot serve as an invitation to those who seek.

Religion as Covenant of Love

The Covenant is a basic concept of the Old Testament. It
is a free gift of God's merciful love: a gift to His people, to
the individual, insofar as he belongs to the people of the covenant and consents to the essential conditions for remaining

among the people of the covenant. Each individual is affected by the covenant. From each one gratitude and fidelity to the God of the covenant and the people of the covenant are expected. The covenant unites the people and bestows upon each individual a special dignity that elevates him as a person above his cultural environment. But a tendency, which the great prophets in particular opposed, showed itself again and again. By the very fact of religion, the bond with the people could lead to a certain superficiality in personal relationships. An individual was prone to take his salvation for granted simply because of his external membership in the community.

From the very fact that the God of the covenant was honored as the Creator of heaven and earth, there were bonds between all men who were creatures of the same God. But the connection between the religion and the people of the covenant permitted the conscience of the majority to limit their love of neighbor to their own people, since the religion of the covenant separated the people of Israel from other peoples. However, the same religion already possessed strong motives, especially through the prophets, for including other nations in the worship of the one God, at least in the expectation of the future.

It is an essential constituent of the Christian religion to tear down all walls of separation between peoples and cultures. This was also an ardent concern of St. Paul. It is a tragedy, therefore, that historical circumstances and human weakness have again and again provided occasion, even under the New Covenant, for confusing the earthly desires of a people with the Christian religion in such a way that the free personal appropriation of religion, as well as universality, have been brought into question. The two principal causes for such confusion are: (1) the identification of the Roman emperors with their office as Pontifex Maximus — High Priest — even after their Christian baptism; and (2) the Germanic principle of absolute allegiance to the prince. Both poisoned streams flowed together in the unheard-of scandals among the European princes of the sixteenth and seventeenth centuries, who usurped to themselves the right to determine religion without regard for the personal conscience of their subjects.

The decree of Vatican Council II on religious liberty signifies the fundamental seriousness of the situation and offers a positive attempt to rectify it. First, the decree makes a clear distinction between religion and the political spheres, recognizing, on the one hand, the autonomy of the secular world, and, on the other, denying every competence to the state in questions directly touching upon faith and decisions of faith. Secondly, faith is taken in all seriousness so that the community of faith and cult rests only on the free decision of faith, which is established through the word and love of Christ. The word of God and the witness of a faith active in love are strong enough to unite the faithful and to invite all men to this unity. This real "power" of religion must not be obscured by an attempt to hold together the community of religion with purely human, political, national, or other temporal means.

If religion, insofar as it is allied with temporal powers and utilized by these powers for their own goals, becomes a cause of separation and antagonism in the world, then the religious community founded on God's word and love is obliged to become a unifying factor from its own innate power, over and above the actions of individual members of its visible community. This power arises from the fact that the Catholic Church in our time of pluralism is freed from temporal commitments; that she considers with loving eyes and in the spirit of adoration everything that God works, even in those parts of Christianity separated from Rome. The Decree on Ecumenism expresses this religious confrontation, which is unhampered by any of the sociological obstacles of the past.

43

The same spirit is expressed in the Declaration on the Non-Christian Religions. The unifying element is first considered in relation to them also, because it is the work of God — before the dividing principle is taken up — which is the work of man. Similarly, the Constitution on the Church in the Modern World sees a thoroughly positive relationship to progress and, in general, to modern culture, since the uniqueness of the Christian religion and, consequently, the relative autonomy of the temporal spheres are more consciously and clearly delineated. Everything that is good is the work of God; we owe Him worship for it.

In summary, we could well brave the thesis: The more religion realizes its ownness as the community of faith, cult, and love, then the more religious decision and the entire religious attitude is the expression of personal freedom. Consequently, solidarity and the absolute respect of freedom in religion will be reflected more fully in the secular sphere, without infringing upon its special character and freedom.

Unity and Diversity of Religion and Morality

In the experience of many men in our worldly world of today, it is quite possible that religion and morality go their separate ways. There are morals of widely varied structures. Today, there is the decidedly moral man who is not religious, or who gives no evidence of belonging to a formal religion. There can be the moral of self-perfection, of the preservation of one's own dignity and honor, as well as a moral that is undoubtedly opposed to the needs of others. A moral of conformity also is possible, in the sense of choosing the more attractive forms of conduct in the environment. There is also the moral that takes its principal guidance from legal science and the administration of laws. If a person with one of these moral commitments enters the sphere of faith, then, his formation of conscience, particularly that which is still recognized as valid in faith, is religiously sanctioned. In conscience and outlook, however, such a person follows his former moral attitude. Moral and religion compose a unity, although moral itself is not yet intrinsically related to religion. However, because the man who has now become a believer also fulfills his moral principles from a religious conscience, one may then speak of "an ethos sanctioned by religion" (Rudolf Otto).

A similar synthesis occurred among the people of Israel when they received the covenant. Much of their original moral content came from the tradition of the environment. With the making of the covenant, the laws and moral judgments already accepted by the people received a higher sanction by the people's membership in the covenant. However, a long period of time was required before the moral concepts of the people of Israel were transformed by the lofty view of the covenant; by faith and worship. In this transformation we observe an infinitely patient and yet ever active divine pedagogy, which has ever repeated itself. We have only to think of how many elements of the Old Germanic and Old Roman tradition went into the making of the Christian moral and were gradually, intrinsically transformed. Is there not a similar confrontation between today's American culture and the Christian religion in its various forms?

Christian ethicians and preachers of moral were not always successful in definitely conceiving and expressing moral in accordance with the form and content of faith and the community of love. The dichotomy between religion and moral received its classic expression in the words that Paul Claudel placed on the lips of his Christian contemporaries: "Certainly we love Christ, but nothing in the world can help us to love moral." Such an expression was meant to depict a legalistic moral colored by many additions from the museum of the past centuries. Man could not find Christ in this morality.

45

It is one of the most important and compelling tasks of the religious renewal of our era to emphasize clearly the unity of religion and religious moral, while paying due attention to the differences involved. A personalistic religion calls for a personalistic understanding of moral in such a way that religion and moral become a whole in the living man.

Christ, the Fulfillment of the "Law"

If by moralists we mean, according to the experiences of the last two centuries, a caste of men who earn their living by classifying moral principles and offering solutions to moral questions, then Christ is not a moralist. Christ is the conqueror of moralism. In Him everything is Good News, and the moral appeal is but a part of the same. He reveals in His own life the most complete unity between adoring love (religion) and obedient redeeming love directed to His fellowman (moral).

God's glory and holiness are unfolded in the mystery of Redemption, in the mystery of Christ. In Christ the full extent of the mystery of God is made manifest: God is Infinite Love. His glory is totally and utterly loving majesty. In Christ, love for the Heavenly Father and love for men are unfolded in the harmony of perfect unity. His supreme act in the Paschal mystery is totally loving adoration and loving service to His brethren. So, too, our love of adoration must embrace in humble service Christ's whole company of the redeemed, ". . . in accord with Christ Jesus, that together you may with one voice glorify the God and Father of our Lord Jesus Christ" (Rom. 15:5-6).

The unity between religion and moral, without the disintegration of religion into moral, has perhaps nowhere found a more perfect expression than in the farewell addresses of Jesus, as given in the Gospel of St. John (cf. 13-17). The fundamental invitation expresses the essence of religion:

"Abide in me, and I in you. . . . As the Father has loved me, so have I loved you. . . . These things I have spoken to you, that my joy may be in you, and that your joy may be full" (15:4, 9, 11). But with the utmost dynamism, the mystery of oneness with Christ and in Him with the Father finds its fruitfulness in brotherly love. Brotherly love follows from the real confrontation with Him Who is Incarnate Love: "He who abides in me, and I in him, he it is that bears much fruit" (15:5). "By this my Father is glorified, that you bear much fruit, and so prove to be my disciples" (15:8). "This is my command, that you love another as I have loved you" (15:12).

Christ compares the harmonious unity of love for Him (and hence for the Father) and love for one's neighbor with His own oneness with the Father and His redeeming love: "If you heed my commands, you will abide in my love, just as I have heeded my Father's commands and abide in His love" (15:10). The Father's "command" to the Son is to reveal the length and the breadth, the heighth and the depth of His love for men, in a love that is limitless. He glorifies the Father precisely through this redeeming love of men. From the oneness — from the *re-ligio* — with Christ there results, with absolute clarity and impelling power, love for all fellowmen.

Morality as Love of One's Neighbor and Responsibility

If the fundamental reality of the Christian religion is the covenant of love, or community with God, then the essential fruit of religion is morality of love for one's neighbor, the community of men in word and love, but a community that is wholly assumed into the religious reality. In a religious affiliation with Christ there is the appeal: "Love one another." The act of living faith changes the interior of man, renews it, and hence renews interhuman relationships.

47

The religious moral and its absolute earnestness result from God's preoccupation with man. When God invites everyone to community with Himself, then all so called must feel impelled to be one before God, to glorify God by their harmony. If community with God means salvation, the living community of men with each other must be experienced as a precious fruit of this salvation — of redemption — and at the same time as an unconditional requirement for salvation.

Religion in its innermost being signifies a personal relationship between God and man. On the other hand, religious moral is an interhuman relationship, but in such a way that it reflects the relationship between God and man. We could say that religious attitude is response to God's word and love. It is directly faced with God Himself. The moral life is a response-responsibility to one's fellowman, the community of men, and all earthly goods and tasks, in order to give God a full and lively response.

The believer detects in the created world and, above all, in his neighbor a message of the Lord, Creator and Redeemer. The sons and daughters of God hear in all things, but especially in all persons, an appeal from the Father. The moral order is concerned with man as the image of God. Therefore, the religious attitude — the relationship with God — should be reflected within the world of men. Moral responsibility makes moral attitudes and decisions a real response to God precisely to the extent that man takes his earthly tasks seriously and accepts earnestly the order of created values. This is achieved in view of his fellowman and finally in view of God, Who calls through these values and through these persons and thus puts man to the test.

The core of moral decision is the spirit of loving obedience to God. It is the saying of "yes" to God's loving Will. But this decision is more than a simple "yes" or "no" to God. Because of his love for God, man makes a personal and a communal effort to discover the proper response that should be made to God through human relationships and activities. The moral decision requires humble attention to the Will of God and hence to one's own possibilities, to the needs of one's neighbor, to the needs of the true brotherhood of men in all fields of life. Man has to make his own decision. Often it may be a bold choice among several possibilities, but it should never be an arbitrary choice. Responsibility means the effort to make a choice that can be offered to God as a response to His love as Creator and Redeemer, a choice that builds up the brotherhood of free persons to the glory of God.

The Content of Responsibility

We understand Christian morality as responsibility in the sense that the Christian, in his relationships to himself, to his human world, to the world of creatures, perceives a word and a message that ultimately comes from God. This responsibility requires further that in his thinking, speaking, and acting, in his personal relations, and his shaping of the world, the Christian give a fitting reply, that he act responsibly so that everything in the last analysis becomes a response that is worthy to be offered to God the Father of all men.

For what then is man responsible? He is responsible for everything that confronts him, everything about which he can freely form his own view.

First, there is man's own self, which must be grasped in the light of his personalism. It cannot be a selfish concern for the self, nor a perpetual regard for the "I," so that the "Thou" is considered only when the "I" is in need. Such a consistent "I-centered" outlook does not allow man to achieve the most profound dimension in his personness. In the question of responsibility to self, only that self is intended that finds itself truly open to the "Thou." Therefore, the healthy regard for the self lies in the examination of conscience concerning the manner in which we have used his gifts and potentialities in relation to his fellowmen and before God. Even in this necessary concern for the "I," man must ever be conscious of his responsive and responsible self, in his self-discipline, and concern for spiritual maturity and personal freedom. Man's responsibility for his own liberty means that liberty that is open to service for the "Thou," the liberty that is open to the word that originates from the "Thou" and is directed to the "Thou" and is devoid of all selfishness, blindness of value, and unjust involvement.

This knowledge of self is the key to the understanding of the primacy of self-responsibility over coresponsibility for our fellowman. We must first remove the beam from our own eye — everything that impedes our loving regard for the "thou," and the "we" — before we can be concerned about the splinter in our neighbor's eye.

Self-responsibility demands that we treat our own individuality with complete seriousness. Even for the good of our fellowman we must not permit ourselves to be reduced to mere numbers. We are obliged to discover our own name and preserve it. Self-responsibility is fidelity to oneself in dialogue with the "Thou." This fidelity or continuity, however, must not be confused with immobility. The best way of remaining loyal to self is in perpetual conversion, the unrelenting effort to attain an ever better disposition to listen, respond, and love.

Since the person can truly "have presence" to himself and others only in word and love, responsibility implies from its very essence the determination for complete being-true in thought, speech, and action. The word must not become like a worn coin or imitation goods. There can be no truly personal existence or being-with without the individual's effort and without the common effort of allies for an ever greater recognition of truth and an ever better way of caring for the community in truth. Because of the incomplete knowledge of man this necessarily includes humility, docility, patience, and respect for others.

Furthermore, the person has to be responsible for his own loving and, within the bounds of his own potentiality, the capacity to love of the "thou" as well. This means, not least of all, attention to spontaneity, gratitude, joy, sorrow, and contrition after refusal. It means also the loving attempt to uncover the hidden and at times buried potentialities of the other's, as well as one's own, heart.

Since man expresses and develops his personness in an already formed proximate and remote environment, his love and responsibility are related to forming the structures of his whole life. These structures include the private and public spheres; economic, cultural, social, and civil life without which the spirit of liberty, and the development of conscience, knowledge, and ultimately genuine love cannot thrive. This principle of structural responsibility does not allow an individualistic situational ethics or unprincipled love ethics. Love must always seek for that order of love that is the best achievable at the moment.

Responsibility for justice, honor, dignity, and respect for those in public life; for cultural progress and worthwhile legislation; above all for the formation of sound public opinion is the special task of the social and religious elite. To use biblical language, responsibility must be a special concern of those who have received two or five talents. The choice of a profession must also be viewed in this light. Everyone should take that place in society where he can do the most good, in view of his particular talents as well as the possibilities and needs of the times.

A particular mode of responsibility is demanded of those in authority. The more intimate and personal the society, the more authority has to express itself as a service of ardent love. And the first goal of authority must be to summon those subject to authority to a responsible, active obedience and to keep open the widest area possible for the realization of this responsibility.

Confronted by the frightening experience of irresponsible obedience by a mass of men — including Christians — to a criminal authority, every thinking man understands today better than ever before that obedience must also be responsible. Obedience must not degenerate to slavish subjection and blind fulfillment of every kind of command. Obedience must not be made less responsible than disobedience, especially when faced with an authority that all too often shrouds itself in the mantle of irresponsibility and lack of spirit.

The world of today beckons to the person who judges and acts from the knowledge of the value content of his actions.

CHAPTER III

Conscience and Freedom

To speak of personalism and existentialism is to speak of conscience and liberty: the two words most dear to our contemporaries. The complete recognition of them and of their underlying values permits dialogue between individuals as well as a serious commitment among communities of persons, and, not least of all, genuinely personal life together in a pluralistic age. Liberty and conscience and the relatedness of these two realities to each other are the bridges by which the faithful can maintain contact with the secular world, in dialogue with all men of good-will.

Conscience and freedom are fundamental Christian values. However, this does not mean that everyone who calls himself a Christian witnesses a greater depth of conscience and realizes freedom more fully than does a non-Christian. But, by his very vocation, a Christian is particularly dedicated to these values and must appreciate the personal and conjoint efforts of all who live, protect, and promote them.

Much in the modern world has contributed to awakening a more passionate love for the basic values of conscience and freedom. The constant threat to their integrity through systems such as Nazism and Communism, which trampled underfoot freedom and personal conscience, has been a wholesome shock. The free world has learned that the future, the coming of age of humanity, depends crucially upon a right understanding and effective protection of these values.

Let us consider the meaning of conscience and freedom and their mutual relationship.

Phenomenology of Conscience

The importance of conscience has never been realized to the same degree by every man in every age. There is even less uniform understanding of conscience or of the proper manner of showing conscientiousness. Modern man invokes conscience at every turn, but what does he understand by it?

The Conscience of the Conformist

The Marxist who adopts every change in the party line declares that the grounds for his fidelity are the ties of his conscience to party unity and historical evolution. In the most profound reaches of his consciousness he fears the sanctions that befall the nonconformist. At the superficial level of his thought he justifies his conduct with ideological reasons. Are there not similar examples of conscience in almost all organizations, in many families, even in churches?

Knowledge about the Value of Obedience and Authority

In addition to an awareness that it is good to adapt oneself to one's environment there can also exist a certain value conception of obedience. For example, usually one person bears the responsibility of decision for the community. On principle, the people under him trust him. Their conscience then adds the commitment of obedience to him. This commitment can reach a point where human behavior patterns and moral values are viewed principally under the aspect of obedience to human authority. A classical realization of this concept is the Old Germanic formula of absolute allegiance to the prince. The brave man followed his prince, no matter

54

what he undertook, even if the follower himself was thereby exposed to the greatest personal dangers. The principle of absolute allegiance played no small role in the Christianization of the Germanic tribes. When the prince became a Christian, the members of his tribe followed him with complete trust. Trust in Christianity was already contained in their awareness of trust in the tribal ruler. Eventually, trust in God largely sublimated this relation of trust and obedience between subject and ruler. In such a world whoever severed solidarity with the ruler was made to seem lacking in conscience. No effort was made to evaluate the motives of the individual or the justice of the ruler's commands. The high churchman who imposes a public oath of absolute allegiance on the priest who disagrees with him follows these same patterns.

If the ethic of absolute allegiance looks to the community and its ruler, then a legalistic conscientiousness concentrates on the abstract formulation of the law. The latter type of conscience follows a very different pattern, depending on whether conformity to the law is based on a legalistic reading of its function or whether the justice of the legislation is considered in terms of human values.

Seventeenth-century moral treatises on conscience devote all of their attention to the binding power of certain doubtful laws and the freedom inherent in others. Behind such treatises there exists a respect for God as Legislator and a disproportionate, fearful respect for the absolute ruler. Some of the best moralists of that era not only had a great esteem for the law, but also were acutely aware that conscience needs an area of freedom in which to confront the values of initiative and creative love. The rigoristic legal attitude recognizes only conscientiousness toward legal formulations; such conscientiousness leads to scrupulosity; a clinging to the meaningless letter of the law and blindness to personal values.

Authority has had a continuing role in the awakening of

conscience. The kind of authority has been the deciding factor. Parents who are the authors of life and who continue their procreative love in deep respect and love for the child awaken in him the awareness that it is good for him to obey their wise and loving guidance. The situation of the child in relation to the development of his conscience is especially fortunate if his parents provide genuine, honest answers to his questioning and openly admit their imperfections and mistakes. Imperfection, humbly acknowledged by good parents, erects a genuine approach to the realization: "Only one is wholly good — God." Thus, by true parental authority the child first meets the world of values.

The Mature and the Immature Conscience

In one period of human history, when leadership was left to the few and the others surrendered themselves unthinkingly, the moral conscience appeared clothed in precisely this paternalism. Within this frame of mind people still developed a deep personal relation to God and the good, but the relation was achieved precisely within the controlling image of the paternal legislator. In our own day, when it is recognized that everyone has his share of responsibility not only for private but also for public life, conscience is now more than ever a question of both personal and community-creative responsibility. However, it would be an oversimplification if we were to adduce the advance to a mature conscience chiefly from the development of human history. The greatest intervention in history was the coming of the Incarnate Son of God. For history, the greatest event is the freedom for which He redeemed man. In the solemn proclamation of His New Law at the Last Supper the Lord said to His Apostles: "No longer do I call you servants, because the servant does not know what his master does. But I have called you friends because all things that I have heard from My Father I have made known to you" (John 15:15). However, there are moments in history and environmental circumstances when the moral corresponding to this word is more hindered than promoted or merely rendered lip service.

The fully developed Christian conscience is inseparable from a loving regard for one's neighbor and a presence before God in faith and love. In the typically Christian, personalistic conscience, God is first encountered, not by means of a law but immediately, in His Self-Revelation, in the communication of His Love. The love that God offers man appeals to him in the midst and the depth of his being, and in such a way that man thereby realizes how closely his salvation depends on his reply to this love. (Salvation here means not only an other-worldly experience of salvation, but also the experiencing of "being healed," of completeness, of the true fulfillment of one's own person.) The mature conscience experiences God as father, friend, fullness of wisdom; as leader and legislator. The decisive element here is that the law rises out of the experience of the wisdom and the love of God, of the personal confrontation with God. The fully developed personal conscience is awareness of the dynamic presence of Him Who calls man in being-one's-self and to being-one's-self. Conscience unfolds itself in the hearing of the Word, which is developed as an appeal to love in return.

Conscience and Faith

The personal make-up of conscience comprises an intrinsic relation between faith and conscience. Faith as a message of love, which beatifies and proclaims the person in his most interior dimension, addresses and animates the conscience, the radical foundation of the person. Ultimately, faith is engaged, not in abstract truths but with Him Who is Truth and Love. All individual truths have their meaning in their relation to the Self-Revelation of God. In living faith man not only opens his intellect to individual truths, but also receives the revelation of Love and surrenders himself joyfully to the Self-revealing God. Thus, he lives from the Word of God. Hence, faith not only addresses conscience but is itself the highest vital expression of conscience. To act from conscience, from honest conviction, or from faith are realities that profoundly complement and illumine each other: ". . . for all that is not from faith is sin" (Rom. 14:23). Faith here means purity and sincerity of conscience.

The Living Conscience of the Anonymous Christian

Without doubt there are men who, though they have not attained Christianity, could yet put many Christians to shame by the vitality of their conscience. They are not only conscientious toward laws and legal minutiae, but they also reveal an astonishing openness for the values of justice, absolute honesty, goodness, joy, friendliness and beauty. They have a conscience for what constitutes and promotes not only their own dignity but also that of their neighbor. Their conscience is in a real sense personal. It is open for the "thou" and for every chance of being enriched interiorly by the "thou" of another, by the community. They are open to promote the good together with their neighbor. They believe in the absolute validity of an order of values from an intrinsic affinity for the good. Even if they had not reached the stage where they can express conceptually the truth about a personal God, everything created serves them as a message of love and an appeal to reply in reverence and gratitude. In a word, they have a conscience that ultimately is a loving openness of the person for his neighbor and for the Other, the absolute Person.

The higher values appeal to man's capacity to love, because they are in their own meaning understood as a message of love, although not in explicit concepts. Both a value ethic and a law ethic are, in the final analysis, based on the fundamental reality of a conscience in which the freedom of the person cannot be overlooked. Both disclose a personally structured world. But only the value ethic reveals a fully developed personalism, which is real encounter in word and love.

A value ethic loses its ultimate meaningfulness if it is denied on principle — as by Nikolai Hartmann and others — that behind the values and the order of values is an absolute Value-Person; if values are broken down into abstractions and abstract principles that man, the "I," can dispose of arrogantly. In such a view conscience becomes a mere reflection of the person's self in his asserted superiority over the impersonal world of values. In real experience of values, however, conscience reveals itself as a profound knowledge of one's self when it is appealed to by the "Thou," by a message of love, purity, humility, justice, and truth that presuppose a "Thou" in absolute perfection.

Conscience shows varied depths, accordingly as the causes for its being aroused by the experience of guilt result from the violation of an abstract commandment, fear of the legislator, or the infringement of a value. The conscience of the Christian personalist, the believer in the true sense, becomes more manifest in confrontation with the human "thou" and in the growing awareness that behind the "I-thou" relation to one's neighbor there is the intensely loving, the truthful, the faithful God.

Freedom

Like the personal interpretation of conscience and having a conscience, so also freedom and the self-understanding of freedom admit of wide range of differences among different men.

Man's freedom comprises a whole that is composed of many individual values. We speak of the civil liberty of each person, the absolute respect of the fundamental rights of all persons in the state; the freedom of the family, of the smaller and basic communities in comparison with the all-embracing whole; the freedom of a nation from suppression by another. Above all, we mean the freedom from unworthy dependence, whether in bare conformism without interior convictions or a blind or slavish obedience that does not sufficiently respect the dignity of the person.

Moral freedom essentially signifies the right and the possibility of following one's own conscience. This means to search freely after the truth and to determine and do freely what one has recognized as good. Moral freedom cannot be understood without considering conscience.

The highest degree of human freedom is the freedom of the sons and daughters of God. It means complete openness for the gift of God's love and complete readiness to undertake the good, not with an eye to rewards or penalties but to the gifts of God. In the freedom of the children of God man has fully surrendered himself to God for selfless service to his brother and to the community. The freedom of the children of God is not faced simply with an impersonal law and impersonal values. Their freedom is the fruit of loving dialogue, of humble hearing, and of gratefully loving response. In the freedom of the children of God it is the power of the love of God that has liberated the heart of man for love. This kind of freedom may seem to denote a certain passivity, since it is freedom in receiving and with a view to receiving. At the same time, however, because total dependence on God is a loving, inwardly affirmed dependence, it means the highest degree of initiative and spontaneity. In the freedom of the children of God man participates in the highest possible degree in the freedom and initiative of God. The freedom of the children of God is also the highest development of the human conscience; the highest sensitivity for the appeal issuing forth from the "Thou"; and the finest perception that the perfection of one's own "I" depends on this openness. In the freedom of the sons and daughters of God we find the most complete synthesis of freedom, authority, obedience, and initiative in the plenitude of a truly alert conscience.

Freedom to Follow the Erroneous Conscience

In the sense that conscience wills and acts in comformity with moral knowing, it can be said to be impervious to error. Conscience is the all-embracing call to honesty. It calls upon man to search untiringly after the true and good. Since, however, man is always a viator — one constantly on the way — he must at times love and do good only insofar as he knows it in his incomplete state.

Therefore, it is not through conscience taken in its entirety but rather in the judgment about the present good that man can, and often does, err. Error can be the expression of superficiality or negligence in the quest for truth. Insofar as man becomes aware of his negligence and still does not make appropriate efforts to come closer to the truth, then he is acting against his better conscience. Error is often caused by environmental prejudices uncritically accepted. A person can rid himself of these prejudices in time, often with the help of enlightened men and women. The more the individual's conscience is respected and the more man's whole education is directed toward acting from a sincere conscience, then the more will personalities develop who can free themselves and others from ingrained prejudices. If conscience is truly honored, today's pluralistic society can spur progress in moral knowledge.

It is a fundamental principle of Christian ethics that man has to follow the judgment of his conscience, even when it is in error. He may not know that it is in error, although he may be aware of the imperfection of his judgment. If his conscience judges sincerely, man's knowledge is for him here and now the best possible approximation to the truth. We have to distinguish, therefore, between a real judgment of conscience and a superficial opinion, which by no means excludes the probability of error and goes hand in hand with negligence in the quest after truth. If, however, it is a question of the best possible knowledge of the good here and now for man, then Cardinal John Henry Newman's saying is absolutely valid: "I have always contended that obedience, even to an erring conscience, is the way to gain light" (*Apologia pro Vita Sua*).

Intolerance has recourse again and again to the principle that "error has no rights." If one concludes from this that another whose convictions are considered erroneous can be persecuted or forced to act against his conscience, then a double error is committed: (1) The abstract order is confused with the reality of the person, who is always in the process of attaining full truth; and (2) One's own convictions are often identified with the truth, and thus one is guilty of idol worship, for God alone is Truth.

Fanaticism, which is bent upon forcing others to act against their conscience, fails against the personal order of things and the truly moral way, for only that which derives from the innermost core of the person, from his full affirmation of the good, is morally good.

If someone is convinced that another follows an erroneous conscience, then it is a demand of love to help him reach the truth according to the measure of prudence, that is, human possibility. This mutual help is the more effective, the more all those engaged therein are aware that they themselves are still in the process of attaining more complete truth. No one has a monopoly on truth. Not even the magisterium of the Catholic Church makes a distinctionless claim to such a monopoly for itself. First of all, those who occupy the magisterium realize that an important source of their own knowledge is the *sensus fidei* of the whole people of God. Secondly, they know that they can teach infallibly only when God Himself has spoken and only by means of the special assistance of the Holy Spirit.

Even when it is a question of the infallible magisterium of the church, the entire people of God must strive constantly to understand this truth more deeply and to express it in the best possible manner, having due regard for various times and cultures. The more the church is aware of her own limitations and the more she refrains from allotting a higher degree to her teaching than is its due, then the more the church will be a bulwark of truth.

The church does not always teach infallibly. A property of a well-trained conscience is that it is satisfied with that degree of certitude attainable under given circumstances. This holds true also for those who wish to enlighten the conscience of men. It is reasonable for the church to orient the conscience of men prudently, even when she does not have infallible certitude at her disposal. This orientation will be all the more beneficial, the more it results from the common effort of the people of God. However, the church's effort does not end here. Rather, it takes seriously all good that appears in the world. Frequently in directing consciences the task of the church consists chiefly in integrating into the view of salvation those values that already have been recognized by men. Still, the church always bases its formation of conscience on absolute respect for the sincerity of thought and action, for acting from one's own conscience.

The Indispensability of the Personal Conscience

It staggers the imagination to think that an earthly authority or an ecclesiastical magisterium could take away from man his own decision of conscience. Every individual man is not only a bearer of general essential properties but also a unique stamp of the same, incommunicable values. Each man views the world in a special way; each has special opportunities for watching over particular values and duties, especially those that correspond to his place in history. Only deference to everyone's conscience and fidelity to one's own conscience make it possible to realize the world of moral values in all its richness. This deference must control not only the relation between individuals but also the social relations between groups.

Vatican Council II has manifested to the world that a very extensive pluralism exists within the Catholic Church. Unity is not necessarily endangered when different conceptions and points of view prevail. Human moral progress is hardly conceivable without occasional tensions among various camps and schools of thought. The moral factor must be proved to a large extent in life.

The pastoral Constitution of the Church in the Modern World (art. 43) speaks of an altogether normal situation, namely, that when Christians are confronted by new and difficult problems they seek a solution in complete sincerity of conscience and conscientiousness among various schools of thought and thereby attain to differences of opinion among themselves. In so doing it is of the utmost importance that no individual and no group presume to identify their own convictions with the Good News of the Gospel or with the natural law. It is precisely the complete candor of conviction together with humility and absolute deference for the others' convictions of conscience that provide the best prerequisite for that fruitful dialogue in which conscience gains more and more light. Thus, the depth of conscience will reveal itself principally through the fact that all those involved in a search for conscience are concerned with the truth and welfare of all.

Religious Freedom

Respect for religious freedom is the decisive test of deference for one's conscience and especially for the truth of the Gospel. If the required condition for religious tolerance were indifference toward the true and the good, not only this question but man's whole life would be trivial and irrelevant. The principle of religious freedom is based on the firm conviction that man is obliged in conscience to strive after the truth and to act according to the truth as he knows it.

From the viewpoint of the believing Christian, religious freedom is posed in the following light: the revealed Word of God is focused on the free man. With the revelation of His love, God does not intend men to be coerced slaves, but friends, sons and daughters, who are filled with truth, with light, and with joy. The revelation of God's truth is so excellent that one can hand it on only by the witness of joyous fulfillment, never by human chicanery or force. For a Christian to act against religious freedom is itself a sign of an unenlightened and defective faith. Often it is actual disbelief, a denial, at least implicit, of the power of grace and the Gospel. As with faith in the Gospel, so also faith in man as the image and likeness of God and as a free person capable of love and truth forbids all conduct that diminishes religious freedom.

The church bears witness to the truth only as a community that incorporates true freedom in genuine conscientiousness and complete deference for the conscience of others. The church is a community of faith under the Word of God and not a religious society under the threat of the sword. Ecclesiastical authority is an authority of love that serves to educate the free person to genuine conscientiousness in profound knowledge of Christ and the moral values.

The church is deeply concerned about the unity of all men in faith. But it is precisely this concern that forbids her to do anything that would be detrimental to conscience. For unity in faith implies the "yes" from the depths of conscience on the part of all those who belong to this community. Since the Christian is always in the process of more fully realizing truth and the good, free utterance of opinions furthers the expression of her unity. When conscience is not permitted this freedom, faith is endangered. Unless each expression of faith and the moral norm is examined in the light of its correspondence to the Gospel and the present hour of salvation, the danger exists that such expression may contain within itself all too many elements of prejudice and of past history. Only honest discussion can consistently separate truth and vigilance for present good from the tenacious retention of traditional formulae.

Religious freedom implies noninterference by the state in religious questions. Therefore, Vatican Council II had to do away with a difficult historical lien on church matters that stemmed primarily from the Old Roman and Old Germanic cultures. From Rome came the heritage of emperors who were at the same time high priests and whose religious interests were state directed. Constantine and his successors brought this heritage into the Catholic Church. It thus became the state religion with the advantage of assistance from the emperor but often with the disadvantage of a constant guardianship and a frequent subordination of its interests to the supposed good of the state.

From the Germanic principalities came the idea of absolute allegiance to the prince, which greatly facilitated the christianization of the Germanic tribes. Charlemagne and Otto the Great combined the Germanic and Old Roman Heritage that to some extent benefitted the church but in the long run impeded the growth of real conscientiousness. A thousand years of Christianity did not suffice to purify or christianize the concept of absolute fidelity to secular authority. During the time of the Reformation and Counter-Reformation both elements converged so that it was left to the prince to determine the religion of his subjects. All of Christianity should have cried aloud over such a scandal.

The true role of the state is to assure religious freedom for both the properly understood common good and for religion. It must assure the sphere of liberty — something which is not always easy, for not only the use of force by the state but also the misuse of freedom by power groups seriously harm freedom. The state's assurance of religious liberty does not mean, however, a real disinterestedness toward religion. For religion is one of man's basic constitutive elements, and the state can manifest complete respect for man's religious nature and the social forms of religion without limiting individual and group liberty in the honest pursuit of truth in any way.

The state is directly interested in the alert conscience of its citizens. If deep convictions of conscience prevail, if the necessary laws and measures are intrinsically perceived and followed from conscience, the state has less need to have recourse to hard measures of control and force. If the state acts properly and the various individuals and groups do their best to make these values known in their common social and political life, the sphere of genuine freedom is already assured, since man can then more easily seek after the full truth of religion.

However, the right of all men to freedom of conscience in the quest after the true religion and in the expression of their religious convictions, both as individuals and in community, is binding on themselves as well as on the state. These values must be realized above all in person-to-person relationships. On the one hand, the being-with of persons demands that they help each other to an ever greater knowledge and realization of the truth. On the other hand, it must be clear

CHAPTER IV

A Christian Existentialism
in the Perspective of Salvation History

The Biblical Notion of KAIROS

Modern theology, duly cognizant of the needs of our contemporary world, is in the process of self-renewal under the quickening influence of Sacred Scripture and the liturgy. Consequently, more emphasis is being placed on the historic-salvific structure of Christian existence. This, in turn, marks the life of the church and that of the authentic Christian as no less dynamic than the rapid pulse of modern society.

The state of tension of the Christian living in the old *aion* (the past era of the unredeemed man, still exerting its baneful influence) and at the same time gratuitously received into the new *aion* (the hour of salvation through Christ) also finds expression in the theological virtue of hope. Unfortunately, current manuals of moral theology, reflecting Catholic moral theology of the last two centuries, fail to portray the riches of the community of salvation and the salvific history of hope. This holds true also for the virtue of prudence, which may be defined as the art of adapting our action to the redemptive actions of Christ within the whole history of salvation and in the context of a present salvific community.

The biblical theology of *kairos* (time of favor) as well as the meaning of *hora* (the present hour), so dear to St. John the Evangelist, possess an unusual fecundity for the renewal of moral theology in the perspective of salvation-history as well as a new approach to the virtue of prudence. In view of this fact, we are not satisfied with a critical review of moral theology in general but aim also at exploring the theological meaning of pastoral sociology as an instrument of prudence oriented toward the historical and community perspective of salvation. In a certain sense we like to call this approach a Christian existentialism and personalism.

Prudence as Attention to the KAIROS

The virtue of prudence plays a decisive role both in the ethics of Aristotle, strongly oriented toward political and civic action, and in the moral philosophy of stoicism, always attentive to the spirit of the universe that penetrates all things. Despite their basic social orientation, these two philosophies have given prudence a function distinctly anthropocentric — which means that it is concerned chiefly with the perfection of man and his search for happiness — possessing the characteristics of a monologue rather than a dialogue. On the other hand, their emphasis on prudence protected their particular ethics against the danger of formalism and legalism. In this sense the virtue of prudence was understood in these pre-Christian ethics as a *sense of the real*.

In the case of the Christian there is a new urgency for a serious and sincere approach to reality in all matters of human action and decision. The question remains: Does Christian existentialism merely apply general principles to particular cases? Unquestionably, the prudent man must also follow general principles and norms. Yet prudence penetrates beyond isolated applications of the general notion and general demands of the essence. It explores the inexhaustible riches of the actual conditions of existence and seeks in them the concretely accessible possibilities for accomplishing the good in a meaningful and *ever original manner* (this originality varies greatly with each action in accordance with the moral "genius" of each person). The virtue of prudence helps the individual discover his uniquely personal response to the challenges and opportunities of his existence.[1]

1. Thomas Aquinas, *Summa Theologica*, II-IIae, q. 47, a.3.

Christian morality considers prudence as the open eye that takes cognizance of the objective reality — the *concrete task* allotted to us by God's love — and in genuine reciprocating charity uses these building blocks of external circumstances and reality for the fulfillment of this task. It was St. Augustine who first described the intimate relationship of the virtue of prudence to divine charity:

> Prudence is love that is clearsighted for that which helps it and that which harms it. And we are not treating here of just any love, but of the love for God, supreme good, supreme wisdom and unity: therefore we can describe prudence as this love which knows how to distinguish between that which is favorable to it and that which is an obstacle to it on the way towards God.[2]

In a similar manner, St. Thomas Aquinas states the above truth succinctly: "Prudence can be called love, not essentially, but insofar as love moves to the act of prudence."[3]

Hence, both Augustine and Thomas consider prudence a virtue that, in a most explicit manner, expresses the "itinerant situation" of man. Christian prudence is the action of a love that hopes, of a love that strives with all its strength for the goal, in keeping with the demands of the living reality. This is completely different from the Aristotelian schema, too often simplified as end and means, a schema that leads us to think of the worship of the man of technology (*homo faber*) rather than of the encounter of the mature person (*homo sapien*) with the living reality that challenges him.

Viewed in the light of the biblical notion of *kairos*, the virtue of prudence will appear more authentically Christian. Anthropocentrism, or man-centeredness, will be counteracted most effectively by man's realization of the truth that prudence, in its perfection, consists more in the humble

2. *De Moribus Ecclesiae Catholicae*, Bk. I, Chap. 15, P. 32, Col. 1322.
3. *Summa Theologica*, II-IIae, q. 47, a.1, *ad primum*.

awareness of God's loving and wise providence than in self-sufficient planning. Christian prudence is an "eschatological virtue," that is, a virtue that makes us fully cognizant of the present opportunities in the great perspective of salvation history.

Those virgins are wise who are ready and wide awake for the coming of the bridegroom (cf. Matt. 25:4). During the time interval before the final coming of Our Lord, the kingdom of heaven demands continuous vigilance and detachment: "For the Son of Man will come at a moment when you do not expect it" (Matt. 24:44). In a similar manner St. Peter gives an eschatological basis for the necessity of prudence; yet, precisely in such a way that the orientation toward the final reality, already in process, constantly influences the present moment of salvation: "Be wise and attentive in prayer! The end of all things is at hand" (I Peter 4:7).

Only the spiritual man who completely abandons himself "to the law of the Spirit which is life in Christ Jesus" (Rom. 8:2) is truly prudent and in complete harmony with the desire of all creation for a share in the spiritual freedom of the sons and daughters of God. We may say with St. Paul: "Those who live on the level of the self-centered nature have their outlook formed by it, and that spells death; but those who live on the level of the spirit have the spiritual outlook, and that is life and peace, for the outlook of the self-centered nature is enmity with God. It is not submissive to the law of God; indeed it cannot be; those who live on such a level cannot possibly please God" (Rom. 8:5-8).

The biblical meaning of *kairos*, as well as a corresponding detachment and watchfulness, are true expressions of the spiritual outlook. The assertions of Sacred Scripture regarding *kairos* clearly explain the significance of such an outlook of the Spirit toward personal maturity and the welfare of the entire Christian community. Prudence, according to the theology of *kairos*, is the attitude of the spiritual man who not only recognizes the signs of the time but who, in a truly filial attitude, wholeheartedly embraces the present moment of salvation and its inherent obligations, so unceasingly offered by God.

Christ, the "Yes" to the KAIROS

Koheleth (Ecclesiastes) knows that everything has its time (*its kairos*). "Every thing under the heavens has its time. There is a time to be born and a time to die . . . a time for snatching up and a time for constructing . . . a time for embracing and a time to avoid it . . . a time to be silent and a time to speak" (*Koh*. 3:1–8). Yet, hidden behind this experience there is a certain pessimism: "God has indeed made everything in its time. Even eternity He has placed in the heart of the children of men; and yet man cannot understand the work that God has done from its beginning to its end" (*Koh*. 3:11). Thus the pre-Christian wise man can offer no more than suggestions. He is unable to offer the final solution, which lies in the interaction of eternity with the particular time interval marked by God for each action. This is the situation of man waiting for the fullness of time, in the light of which the final meaning of each time interval prepared by God will become manifest for those who live on the level of a spiritual outlook.

One of the most important messages of Our Lord is that of joy at the approach of the fullness of salvation. The opening of the Gospel — the summary of Christ's preaching according to St. Mark — begins with the solemn announcement that now the *kairos*, the time of salvation that enlightens and challenges men with power, is at hand. After the arrest of John, Jesus returned to Galilee where He proclaimed the Good News prepared by God: "The times are fulfilled and the Kingdom of God is at hand: be totally dedicated and accept the Good News" (Mark 1:14). The *kairos,* the time of salvation *par excellence* predetermined and prepared for by God, had its beginning in the Incarnation of Jesus.

Christ Himself is the bearer of the *kairos* in His first coming, and He shall completely fulfill it in His second coming. In addition, He is the prototype *par excellence* who teaches us how to conduct ourselves in regard to the *kairos.*

In Christ the *kairos* has come: "At the appointed times, God revealed his Word" (His *Logos*) (Titus 1:3), His revelation, which continues in the proclamation of the apostles, in the time of salvation appointed by God (cf. I Tim. 2:6); "in his own time — on that day which the Blessed and Unique Sovereign, the King of Kings and Lord of Lords, will cause to appear at the appointed times" (I Tim. 6:15). This text, from the very start, stresses the sovereignty of God, Who determines His own time. "When we were still in misery, Christ, at the set time, died for those who were separated from God" (Rom 5:6).

Jesus stressed repeatedly that it is the Father in His absolute sovereignty Who has determined the moments of salvation (cf. Acts 1:7). By repeated references to the fact that all His actions were directed by His Father's will, Christ proved that in Him the Kingdom of God had come. He allowed Himself to be guided solely by the will of the Father as expressed in the *kairos.* He is so completely wedded to the divine ways that His entire life is consumed by the desire to accomplish the plan of the Father in complete obedience and self-surrender. His gaze is fixed on the will of the Father, which enables Him to act and reveal Himself at the determined, favorable time (*kairois hidiois*). All of Our Lord's actions were done "in that time" (*en ekeinoi toi kairoi*); namely, in the salutary moment always predetermined by the Father. This is particularly evident in the most important moments of His earthly life; as, for example, at the time of the revelation of the name of God the Father, expressed in His prayer of thanksgiving for God's revelation to those completely dedicated to His glory: "At that time Jesus spoke these words: I praise you, Father, Lord of heaven and earth. . . ." (Matt. 11:25).

In His perfect attitude to His heavenly Father, Jesus is the absolute prototype for His disciples. He is totally turned toward the Father in order to receive from Him the *kairos* in perfect holiness of response. He contrasts His own attitude toward the *kairos* with that of His unbelieving relatives: "My time has not yet come. Your time is always ready. Go to the feast. I am not going because my time is not yet fulfilled" (John 7:6–8). His contemporaries, who were practically unbelievers, made their own decisions, planned their own time and future. Even in the fulfillment of certain obligations of the Law they acted in view of their own considerations rather than at the good pleasure of God; as, for example, in the prescribed pilgrimage to the Temple. Jesus is pre-eminently holy on the level of response, of conformity to "the call of God." In this He fulfills the prophecy of the Servant of Yahweh: "The Lord opens my ear each morning, in order that I may listen to him as a disciple. The Lord God has opened my ear. And I did not resist, I did not turn my back" (Isa. 50:4–5).

Jesus viewed His entire existence in the light of His *Hour* par excellence (in a certain sense, St. John's meaning of *hora* is particularly close to the meaning of *kairos*). All events of Christ's earthly life are illumined and glorified by the dignity of His death and resurrection in such a manner as to make manifest the Father's plan of love and the fullness of the salvific action. This constant reference to the Father's will and plan is evident at the wedding feast in Cana, when the Lord answered His Mother: "My Hour has not yet come" (John

2:4). Thus, the great moment in which Jesus began His signs and the revelation of His glory (cf. John 2:11) is placed, from its very inception, within the radius of that great Hour that became the turning point in the history of the world: the Hour of the establishment of the Covenant in His blood, the Hour of the revelation of His glory in the Paschal mystery.

The gospel account of the Last Supper, in particular Our Lord's action of washing the feet of His apostles, opens with the deeply significant words: "Because Jesus knew that the time [His *kairos*] had come to go back to his Father" (John 13:1); "As the hour had come" (Luke 22:14). Earlier that day, His message to the proprietor of the Supper Room had been: "My time is at hand. I wish to observe the feast of the Passover with my disciples at your house" (Matt. 26:18). Jesus, deeply cognizant of the significance of that great hour of salvation: ". . . raised his eyes to heaven and said: My Father, the hour has come, glorify your Son in order that your Son may glorify you" (John 17:1). He foresaw the terrible anguish preceding the momentous decision to accept "His Hour." Nevertheless, His response was a total *Yes* of abandonment to His Father's will for that decisive hour. Completely aware of its terrifying implications, Jesus prayed: "What shall I say? Father, deliver me from this hour? *It is for this hour that I have come.* Father, glorify your name" (John 12:27f.). Our Lord's entire life was completely oriented toward this hour. He foresaw in this hour of suffering the hour of salvation for all mankind, Jews as well as Gentiles. When some Greeks desired to see Him, He responded: "The hour has come in which the Son of Man is glorified. Amen I say to you, unless the grain of wheat fall into the ground and die, it remains alone. But if it die, it brings forth much fruit" (John 12:23f.).

77

The Morality of Life in Christ Jesus under the Sign of KAIROS

Saint Mark opens his gospel account with the first sermon of Jesus, which epitomizes His entire message. Its content clearly indicates that the Christian life is under the great sign of the *kairos*, the hour of salvation, which is to be acknowledged and received with humble gratitude. The message of joy is "the *kairos* in its fulfillment," which calls for a response of joy and dedication: "Be totally dedicated [be renewed in your mind] and accept the message which is joy" (Mark 1:15).

In its essence, Paul's letter to the Corinthians is a commentary on the opening of the gospel. His lofty ideals and moral demands are logical conclusions from the *kairos*. In view of the hour of salvation at hand, Paul expected the same detachment from married Christians as from those living in the celibate state. In view of the *kairos* he encouraged those burdened by suffering to rejoice, while he exhorted the more fortunate brethren to keep in mind the time of grace and to bear witness to the fullness of salvation (cf. I Cor. 7:29f.). Similarly, Peter, in his appeal for conversion, urges the Christians to repentance and amendment of life in preparation for Our Lord's second coming (cf. Acts 3:19f.). This bond between *kairos* and conversion is further emphasized by Paul: "At the perfectly fitting time I heard you and in the time of salvation I helped you. Behold, the time desired has arrived; behold, the time of salvation has come" (II Cor. 6:2). In the final analysis the morality of *kairos* is synonymous with the "Law of Grace." Paul, full of zeal in his apostolic vocation, which he considered a humble *collaboration* with the divine salvific action of God, further exhorts his converts: "Do not receive the grace of God in vain" (II Cor. 6:1). This statement emphasizes the importance of grace in this time of salvation. In the same context, he expects a vigilance born of zeal for souls that guards against any type of scandal (cf. II Cor. 6:3).

Kairos is the time of Our Lord's coming: both His first coming, which reached its climax in the Paschal Mystery (the death and resurrection of Christ), and His second coming (the *Parousia*). These salvific events deeply touch each Christian's life by bringing him close to Christ, the divine exemplar, with the perfect attitude of response to His Father's plan of salvation. Our transformation into 'other Christs' is effected chiefly through the sacraments, the efficacious signs of God's salvific action. In a very special way the institution of the Eucharist marked the *hour*, or the *kairos*, for Jesus and His disciples. In a certain sense this sacrament makes us contemporaries of Christ, not by virtue of fleeting time (*chronos*), but according to the hour of grace (*kairos*). Hence, God has called us into existence at the very hour of salvation itself, in view of which a particular moment of grace receives its dynamism. He has called us into the fullness of salvation here and now through the urgency of the *kairos* in Christ's first and second coming. These are two decisive forces and motives for our actions here and now according to the opportunities of each "hour." In baptism the Christian has been integrated into the salvific events of Christ's death and resurrection. In each celebration of the Eucharist he "proclaims the death of the Lord, until he comes" (I Cor. 11:26). Therefore it behooves the Christian that he imitate Christ's response of conformity to "the call of God" in any decisive situation of life and thereby give concrete realization to God's salvific plan.

Thus the Greek notion of *Kairos* formulates for us with a sharpness that is no longer familiar to our religious thought the seriousness of the decision before which we are placed by Jesus in the proclamation of his religious message and by Paul in his moral demands:

the more the end becomes visible in the fulfillment
already present, the stronger becomes the demand of
the *kairos*, a demand renewed at each instant of
Christian existence, and which by this very persistence
demands of the Christian that he be unceasingly
conscious of the *kairos* itself and that he be faithful to
it in its concrete demands, for example, in the
manifestation of fraternal love (cf. Rom. 13:8–11).[4]

To walk in the footsteps of Christ, imitating His loyal response to the *kairos* of each moment, presupposes a close
union with God. This, in turn, is based on vigilance and responsiveness to God's grace in genuine consideration and
concern for the welfare of the neighbor and the community.
This same perspective appears in Our Lord's warning concerning the salvific moment of His return and the frightening
judgment that will precede it: "At every moment [*en panti
kairoi*] be attentive in prayer so that you be prepared for
what must happen and for the meeting with the Son of Man"
(Luke 21:36). Each Christian existence is drawn into the
great salvific event of Our Lord's second coming. Therefore,
a constant watchfulness and openness to the call and grace of
God is required in each moment: "Pray unceasingly, watch
and pray; for you do not know when the *kairos* is coming.
. . . Pay attention; for you do not know when the Lord will
come, so that when he does come, he does not find you sleep-
ing. I say to all of you: be vigilant" (Mark 13:33–37; see
also Luke 12:40).

The time of salvation between the first and the second
coming of Christ forms "the last hour" or interim moment
(cf. I John 2:18) and, as such, demands vigilance and an attitude of responsiveness to God's plans. The Christian should
be an attentive and responsive interpretor of God's providence.

4. Gerhard Delling, "Kairos" in *Theologisches Wörterbuch zum
Neuen Testament,* III, 461.

The very nature of this end-time urgency demands a constant conversion and a renewal of fervor: "And this is important for us who understand the time of salvation [the *kairos*]: now is the hour to awaken from our sleep" (Rom. 13:11).

Even the hour of temptation may be seen by the believer as a *kairos* (cf. Luke 8:13, "the *kairos* of temptation"; Apoc. 3:10, "the hour of temptation"). According to the plan of God's love, this *kairos* must waken the believer from his lethargy and rouse him to action, lead him to prayer, and guide him in grace to the radical choice of the good. Then the Lord will be ready to deliver His own from the hour of temptation.

And all those who, in the light of the fullness of salvation of the *kairos*, renounce everything in order to follow the call of God's will, at that time receive a hundredfold in both joy and suffering. This means that the *kairos* offers them countless opportunities to strengthen their love and render perfect proof of their choice of the Lord (cf. Mark 10:29–31).

Each hour of decision, each *kairos* determined by the Lord, carries in itself the eschatological fullness and the power of the judgment; each must be seen in relation to the great and final hour of judgment, of the separation of the good and the evil (cf. Apoc. 14:7). Thus, the final hour, the hour of judgment, in a very special way becomes the hour of fulfillment for the disciples of Jesus in view of their commitment to the Lord (cf. Apoc. 14:15). In the attitude toward the *kairos* judgment is already beginning and being carried on.

Imbued with the truth that each hour impels us to a sincere decision in the light of the great events of salvation, Peter, speaking of *kairos*, affirms that "the judgment begins in the house of God" (I Peter 4:17). On the one hand, the *kairos* may be seen as a punishment for Christians, God's people, for their failure to live according to the fullness of grace of this end-time. On the other, trials sent by God may be seen as a grace and blessing from the long-suffering God Who unceasingly and urgently invites His own to full renunciation and conversion. For the unbeliever, the *kairos* of judgment in the house of God will sound the warning: "If in fact the judgment is beginning with us, what will be the end of those who do not obey the Gospel?" (I Peter 4:17).

The morality of *kairos* precludes all autonomous planning on the part of man. It runs counter to the Aristotelian anthropocentric attitude that views everything in the perspective of goal (happiness of the individual) and of means toward that goal. Such a perspective may render us unresponsive and neglectful of God's graces. Opposed to this attitude is the morality of the Gospel, which demands vigilance and absolute self-detachment in regard to the concrete opportunities for good prepared by God for each particular hour.

The attitude of response to God's plan, wherein man resists his tendency toward autonomous planning, has nothing in common with quietism. On the contrary, the ethics of *kairos* is truly dynamic, and even demanding, for its power is from God Himself. In the broad context of Paul's Letter to the Galatians, *kairos* takes on a new dimension that emphasizes that the morality of the freedom of the sons and daughters of God is neither sloth nor lawlessness nor arbitrariness: "Let us do good untiringly. If we are not negligent, we shall harvest the fruits in the *kairos*. Hence, in the measure in which the *kairos* permits us, let us do good perfectly toward all but especially toward our brothers in the faith" (6:9). This same exhortation is repeated in the letters to the Ephesians and the Colossians: "Use the present opportunities to the full for these are evil days" (Ephes. 5:16). This means that neglect of opportunities for good is unfortunate because the *kairos* will not be repeated. This characteristic of the *kairos* — as the unique occasion for apostolic activity and fraternal charity — is clearly enunciated by Paul in his epistles to the Colossians and Galatians: "Act wisely toward those from the outside by profiting from the *kairos*" (Col. 4:5).

Such high rewards of *kairos* are accessible to the Christian in relation to Christ and through the Spirit sent by Him.

The Morality of KAIROS and the False Situation-Ethics

There is a danger that persons unfamiliar with Christian morality or having only a superficial knowledge of its principles may confuse the moral perspective of *kairos* (the hour of salvation) with the false tenets of situation-ethics, which in recent years have been condemned repeatedly by the church. Consequently, the question arises whether in our reaction to situation-ethics it would be safer to place greater stress on the precise boundary lines of laws, prohibitions, and restrictions without concern for the *kairos*.

In answer to such a position, it should be pointed out that both the Christian-at-large and the moral theologian must be concerned primarily with ascertaining God's will and word rather than finding the easiest and most expedient way. Undoubtedly we need the minimal boundary lines of law. There are certain minimal demands, clear and obligatory to all. These arise from the order established by a loving Creator and the present economy of salvation. Yet it would be absolutely unfaithful to the *kairos* (the time of the fullness of salvation) to place undue stress on these minimal demands of law. The basic formula of the new Law, "the law of the Spirit of life in Christ Jesus" (Rom 8:2), is the great commandment that impels us unceasingly toward a more perfect love of God and neighbor. The keynote of the Sermon on the Mount is: "Be perfect as your heavenly Father is perfect" (Matt. 5:48). Moreover, the text of the gospel leaves no doubt as to the emphasis of the evangelist, expressed with unsurpassed clarity, that the Sermon on the Mount is the proclamation of the new Law — a law with impelling force — confronting each person in the form of commandments, obligations, duties, responsibilities, and urgings of grace.

Furthermore, it should be remembered that a morality with onesided stress on minimal requirements of law produces the dangerous tendency of leading into false situation-ethics and of preventing a spontaneous and wholehearted effort toward the higher demands of the law of the spirit. Such a onesided morality of minimal demands psychologically attracts men to these limits, like a fence in a pasture attracts animals to pasture near the borderline. Furthermore, the onesided morality of "fences" has been the cause for confusion between the demands of the natural law and the Gospel message on the one hand, and the regulations and ordinances of the positive law on the other. The resulting confusion has contributed to a reaction of false situation-morality.

Positively speaking, we must affirm the fact that the biblical morality of *kairos* is at a directly opposite pole from the false situation-ethics, and that it alone is able to restore unity and harmony to all morality. Moreover, the chief differences between the morality of *kairos* and situation-morality are the following:

1). A difference in *orientation:* The false situation-ethics stresses human freedom, the spirit of independent initiative and autonomous self-realization, beyond the limits of the essential order willed by the Creator and the Savior. It remains close to an ethics of borderline law though it transgresses the law when need is felt. The ethics of *kairos*, on the other hand, is bent uncompromisingly toward the higher demands of love of God and neighbor. This, in turn, disposes the person to greater fidelity in the practice of all the other virtues, which, in their final analysis, are "mediators of love" of God and neighbor.[5]

5. Karl Rahner states succinctly: "Love is not something accomplished once for ever in a definitive way, nor accomplished by sub-

2). A difference in *attitude and fundamental opinion:* The false situation-ethics is an expression of the *sarx,* the selfish man, a prisoner of his own egocentrism, concerned only for his own glory, his independence, and, at best, a self-perfection, poorly understood in a self-centered existentialism. The ethics of *kairos,* on the other hand, is a gift and a realization of the *Pneuma,* the spirit of Christ. It is the ethics of the spiritual man, of the man liberated from the bond of the law to the extent that he permits himself to be led by the Spirit (cf. Gal. 5:18; Rom. 6:14; 8:14), rather than being satisfied with observing minimal standards of law imposed by authority or allowing himself the transgression of essential laws.

The man of the *sarx,* the man who arranges his life in an autonomous fashion, experiences difficulty in subordinating himself even to the minimal demands of the law imposed from without (cf. Rom. 8:3) and, to a far greater extent, in complying with the law of grace. However, the Christian, the spiritual man, who makes the most of the *kairos,* not only fulfills the minimal demands of law but fixes his attention beyond the mere fulfillment to the central aim and objective of the law; namely, the love of Christ.

3). An *individualistic trend:* The situation-ethics of existentialism may be interpreted in an individualistic manner.

stitution. It is never given away but always tends towards its own better realization. . . . It is basically erroneous to reduce love to the fulfillment of all the other commandments" ("Das 'Gebot' der Liebe," in *Schriften zur Theologie,* Band V [Einsiedeln-Zürich-Köln, 1962], p. 508). Rahner also expresses a somewhat related thought: "The readiness to become involved in planning a dynamic future venture is completely different from admitting that tomorrow we must pay a banknote which today is not yet due. He who loves must pledge himself *today* for the adventure of a love which is meant for tomorrow. Yet, he must do the task of today even though he feels that today's challenge is surpassed by that of tomorrow and even though he prepares himself today for tomorrow's demands. Love proves itself genuine only if it constantly strives to perfect itself, only if it is truly in the process of growth or on the way" (*Ibid.,* p. 509).

The ethics of the *kairos*, on the contrary, is essentially oriented toward *community salvation*. It is precisely in the salvific solidarity established by Christ that individuals and communities fulfill their particular *kairos* and thereby contribute to "the upbuilding of the Body which is Christ" (cf. Eph. 4; I Cor. 12).

Some forms of situation ethics can be understood as a reaction against shallow and rigid legalism. But as reactions they are often bound by the very attitudes they oppose. This is especially true in the case of Joseph Fletcher's "Situation Ethics." *The New Morality* (The Westminster Press, Philadelphia, 1966).

(a) Legalism constantly confuses love and justice. Since it does not build on the concept of personal and interpersonal relationships, it does not try to describe the true countenance of love. Joseph Fletcher goes all the way when he asserts: "Love and justice are the same" (*Ibid.*, p.87ff.). "They are one and the same thing and cannot vary" (*Ibid.*, p.89). He does not, however, do justice to most Catholic moralists when he maintains: "All Catholic moralists separate them, making love a 'supernatural' virtue and justice a 'natural' one, holding that we *must* be just in our actions but only *may* be loving!" (p. 93–94). Good Catholic moral theology has always taught that man's highest and most urgent vocation is to love his neighbor and that justice is one of the implications of love.

(b) The legalists made little effort to define their rules or norms in terms of values or in view of human relationships. As a consequence, their too materially worded rules forbade attitudes and acts of various moral values. Joseph Fletcher carefully preserves this carelessness, which seemingly allows him to show that all these norms or rules are open to countless contradictions or exceptions. For instance, neither Fletcher nor the legalists make any effort to study the meaning of language in its total personal and social context.

Otherwise they would realize that the spelling out of truth must be done in view of the partners and their situation. What the legalist condemns as lying, and what Fletcher praises as a loving and good lie, would not be called a lie at all if the total language of communication were more precisely explained in terms of value and in the full context of the persons involved.

(c) Legalism is careless about the necessary distinctions between statutory laws and those moral norms that indicate the "order of love." The typical legalist is also a naive or stubborn "situationist." He equates man-made laws and mere human traditions with moral norms that are directly based on the innermost being and calling of the human person and that express genuine personal and interpersonal values. Hence he ever deserves the reproach: "Why do you break God's commandment in the interest of your traditions?" (Matt.15:3). The modern descendent of such legalistic situation ethics follows the same formalistic tradition. Although he surely does not stress the legal situation, he looks to the vital interest of pragmatic and utilitarian love. For him the moral norms and love itself have no definite meaning. While the legalistic situationist is somehow agnostic through laziness in making distinctions, Fletcher, the modern situationist, again goes all the way. Being an outspoken agnostic, he does not see any ground for distinguishing statutory laws from moral norms expressive of the innermost being of the human person. Fletcher, Bishop Robinson, Marc Oraison, and others rightly insist on the Lord's word: "The Sabbath was made for the sake of man and not man for the Sabbath" (Mark 2:27). But then they apply this to all moral norms: "Morality is made for man and not man for morality." They do not realize that the true meaning of morality and of moral norms is not merely law given to man or imposed upon man, but rather a dynamic orientation "given" by man's own innermost being.

(d) Legalism is a static approach to morality. It concentrates almost all its energies on distinguishing the minimal boundary lines. Its casework engages in minimalism, though it may be very rigid and inflexible. Similarly, Fletcher's situation ethics concentrates almost exclusively on the boundary lines also, although with the intention of leading below those lines. Our approach, on the contrary, is dynamic and concentrates on the discernment of the spirits indicating active norms of growth, leaving space enough for the creativity of the individual person or group, but contained within the "order of love," or at least within a dynamic searching for this order of love. While for Fletcher, love is unprincipled and at the same time a formalistic principle without content — a sphinx without countenance — our approach is oriented toward an understanding of true love and its mediation in and through the whole of morality. As theologians, we do not have to deal with a bare abstract principle of love, but with God Who is Love and Who has shown us the countenance of love in His Son made man, in Christ, our brother.

(e) A static legalism tends to seduce man to self-righteousness. In view of many legal and static rules one may assert: "All these I have observed from my youth" (Mark 10:20). From the implications of Fletcher's situation ethics, one may move toward self-righteousness and static self-satisfaction at even a cheaper price: "Gone is the old legalistic sense of guilt and of cheated ideals when we tailor our ethical cloth to fit the back of each occasion. We are deliberately closing the gap between our overt professions and our covert practices" (*Ibid.*, p. 147). More or less, this frank statement means the "end of the Reformation."

(f) Fletcher's situation ethics outstrips even the legalists in systematic disregard for biblical teaching or in misuse of biblical quotations. Two examples may stand for many others. Speaking on the "brave and responsive decision" of a mother to have an abortion because of a possibility that the embryo might be deformed, Fletcher says: "This was a kairos, a fullness of time" (*Ibid.*, p. 135-36). In the Bible, the kairos is characterized by the loving decision of Christ to suffer for others. Fletcher's "fullness of time" is characterized by using all means to avoid risk of suffering. The teaching of Christ as reported in the Bible seems no longer to be the basis or orientation for theology. He writes: "The fact that Jesus is reported in the Gospel as having blessed David's act (eating the reserved Sacrament) on the basis of the situation, while he also absolutized the prohibition of divorce, poses a problem for Biblical scholars but it does not confuse Christian ethics, at least of the situationist stamp. We are quite clear about it: to will the end is to will the means" (*Ibid.*, p.133). "We find nothing in the teachings of Jesus about the ethics of sex, except adultery and an absolute condemnation of divorce — a correlative matter" (*Ibid.*, p.139).

For me, the first theological question is: What did Christ really teach? What kind of orientation does the Gospel really give us?

The Socio-salvific Dimensions of Kairos

The time of favor, the hour of unrepeated possibilities prepared by God, is a completely personal challenge, yet always mediated in and for the context of community. As seen above, the *kairos*, which the Christian must "redeem" (use to the fullest), involves his personal participation in the *kairos* of Christ and thereby becomes a mission toward the community (cf. Col. 4:5). Furthermore, the *kairos* may directly challenge the community: the community itself is subject to the biblical morality of the *kairos*. The *kairos* of Christ, the new head of mankind, is the time of salvation for the entire family of the redeemed. Consequently, the chosen people of God are also in possession of the *kairos* insofar as it concerns Christ's coming, His preaching, and His manifestations of power.

Our Lord wept over Jerusalem because it "did not know the *kairos* of his visit" (Luke 19:44). Jesus reproached the crowds for their lack of perception for the "signs of salvation at hand," despite their ability to observe the earthly signs and happenings: "You hypocrites, you know how to evaluate the face of the heavens and the earth; how does it happen that you cannot judge the signs of the *kairos*?" (Luke 12:57). The same reproach is aimed particularly at the leaders of the Jewish people: the Pharisees and the Sadducees. They, above all, were in a position to recognize the advent of the great time of salvation by means of Christ's personality and the signs and wonders that He wrought (cf. Matt. 16:1ff.). The Pastoral Constitution On the Church in the World of Today is an effort to evaluate the signs of the time — of today — and to lead to a common action that should be responsive to the present opportunities.

KAIROS and the Sociological Situation

Sociology and, as such, the empirical social sciences are concerned with social facts and phenomena. They look for a science of change and for the evolution of social patterns that clearly reveal the interdependence between religion (morality) and social factors. A chief characteristic of sociology is a search for sociological causes. This, in turn, sometimes may color modern sociology with a decidedly *deterministic note*. To some extent this tendency represents the sociological situation as completely *hopeless*. It is fortunate that today we rarely meet this type of summary "sociologism," which tries to explain everything on the basis of sociological factors acting as relentless elements. At any rate such a sociology seems to have nothing in common with the biblical conception of *kairos*.

However, today's sociology, if unprejudiced, will be aware that the quasi-quantities and the sociological determinisms that may be present are due chiefly to the inevitable consequences of a misguided human freedom that failed to utilize its great potentials.[6]

Both sociology and psychology disprove man's false belief in absolute arbitrary freedom. Nevertheless these sciences have done much to uncover *the ever-present authentic possibilities of the individual and society toward greater freedom in the direction of the good*. It is especially helpful to realize that, without a common pledge for freedom and without a certain investment in freedom, genuine solidarity and freedom in the economic and social structures and in the cultural and intellectual life would be seriously endangered.

These ideas are in full agreement with the biblical concept of *kairos*, even if the latter transcends mere sociological views. Man cannot pretend to be able to realize and actualize good in an a-historic manner by choosing autonomously between thousands of abstract possibilities. Rather, he must humbly explore all the real (sociological) possibilities. These may be limited, modest, but nevertheless real. In the same measure as he actualizes them, new doors of possibilities toward greater progress and freedom are opened before him.

Pastoral Sociology and the Signs of the Times

A more complete realization of the theological value inherent in the doctrine of *kairos* will lead men to a more productive understanding of pastoral sociology. For this reason it is important that not only the moralist but all responsible men should acquire a deeper understanding of sociological factors so vital for the apostolate.[7]

6. Cf. G. Gurvitch, *Déterminismes sociaux and liberté humaine* (Paris, 1955); Bernard Häring, "Auseinandersetzung mit dem Soziologismus; Milieu und Freiheit" in: *Ehe in dieser Zeit* (Salzburg, 1964), pp. 47–72; *Marriage in the Modern World* (Westminster, 1966).
7. Cf. W. Schöllgen, *Die soziologischen Grundlagen der katholischen Sittenlehre* (Düsseldorf, 1953), pp. 9f., 60, 150f., 373. *Idem.*, "Der Heilige Gheist und die Sozialforschung" in: *Lebendige Seelsorge*, 7 (1956), 211–14.

However, this does not imply that the doctrine of *kairos* alone would suffice to establish a theological basis or a practical introduction to the methods employed by empirical sociology in the development of a constructive pastoral theology. Equally important are the other great socio-salvific perspectives; such as, the mystery of the Incarnation and the *incarnate* character of the Christian religion; the relations of the secular world and the Kingdom of God; the salvific solidarity of all men in Adam and, more so, in Christ; the biblical notion of the person with its basic existential categories, such as I-You-We.[8] Finally, it is necessary to have both a correct understanding of the history of salvation and a clear conception of profane history and natural law.

Vatican Council II, deeply rooted in the theology of the Trinity, on the one hand gave witness to Christian unity and, on the other, was distinctly *under the sign of the kairos.* Pope John XXIII's opening discourse at the first session clearly gave the setting for the council's great task of aggiornamento. Pope Paul VI invariably returned to the challenging reality of "the signs of the time." The chief objective of Vatican II, as enunciated by both popes and supported by the Council fathers, was to ascertain the signs of the time — our time. This entails not only the task of entering deeply into the spirit and thought of contemporary men, but, likewise, a respectful attitude toward their ways of thinking, feeling, and acting. Only thus shall we find them receptive to the message of salvation that is suitable to our time, given in a language understood by the people of today. Furthermore, the tone of the council was strongly marked by the experience of unity in diversity and diversity in unity.

Beginning with the constitution on the renewal of the liturgy, the church realized its mission of becoming all things to all people. By meeting the needs of the people of various

8. Cf. Häring, *Macht und Ohnmacht der Religion,* 2nd ed. (Salzburg, 1957).

cultures, races, and language differences, she made the riches of the liturgy accessible to all in order to lead men to share in community the full joys of the liturgical functions. All these aspects are particularly manifest in the Pastoral Constitution on the Church in the World of Today.

At this turning point in history the church of Vatican II, in a truly authentic spirit of Catholicity and imbued with impartial love for all, gathers men of different cultures to share in its doctrine, its morality, its liturgy and pastoral love. The union of so many different cultures within one and the same church proves that man is to some extent a product of his particular epoch though he comes from God and is on pilgrimage toward an eternal home. Consequently, it should be natural for man to act in conformity with history as with the other exigencies of the *lex naturae* (of the natural moral law). To act in conformity with history constitutes one of the constant demands on human nature: of acting as a human being and of maintaining authentic fidelity to the total vocation of man.[9] This also is a basis for ecumenism (cf. Decree on Ecumenism, Arts. 9, 10, 11, 17!).

We must keep in tune with the pulse beat of our age and scrutinize the signs of the times and interpret them in the light of the Gospel. In this sense we may say that pastoral sociology has its *kairos* today. It is important that this fact be recognized and utilized to the fullest extent. We are aware that pastoral sociology is of paramount importance in today's dynamic, competitive, and pluralistic society, whereas, in primitive, static societies the wisdom of the sages might have sufficed.

Today it would be imprudent to forego the insights and tools derived from such social sciences as experimental soci-

9. Cf. J. Fuchs, "Naturrecht und positives Recht" in *Stimmen der Zeit* 163 (1958–1959), 130–41, *Idem.; Lex naturae – Zur Theologie des Naturrechts* (Düsseldorf, 1955). Cf. also Häring, "Man in History" in: *The Law of Christ* (Westminster, 1966), I, 87–92, 287–308.

ology and social psychology. They investigate causal relationships and point out new approaches in the solution of problems. They contribute to an objective evaluation and possible
solution of mutual problems by an assiduous study of the
particular spirit of the time and its relevance to truth and absolute moral demands. The reciprocal relationship between
religion — the moral religious life of the individual and society — and economic, cultural, and political forces, must be
explored fully and put to the task of world improvement and
church reforms.

Nevertheless, it is important to note here that empirical
sociology alone is incapable of formulating a Christian understanding of the signs of the times in terms of the *kairos*. Experience alone cannot be the sole measure of things. Therefore, empirical pastoral sociology is a subordinate science,
similar to all modern methods of historical research in church
history. In the sociological sense it is a science of empirical
approach. It must face the facts with real serious-mindedness.
Unless the factual data are adequate, the signs of the times
cannot be interpreted in a meaningful manner toward a wise
pastoral plan that is close to reality. At the same time we
must remember that, ultimately, sociological facts must be interpreted in the light of theology, *under the sign of faith*. To
empirical research we must add the investigation of the the-
ological-pastoral meaning of the situation. Therefore, we
may say that *only he who is truly enlightened by faith and
the gift of wisdom is able to use the materials of sociological
research for a pertinent interpretation of the signs of the
times.*

Hence, a precise distinction must be made between empirical sociological research and theological knowledge. While
pastoral sociology should utilize all available scientific means,
the evaluation and selection of means must be made under
the inspiration of faith.

Only by adopting such an attitude, as imposed by the

biblical doctrine of *kairos*, are we able to study the signs of our times, evaluate the sociological factors, and comprehend our responsibilities in making the decisions that our time demands.

Only if the *kairos* determines Christian morality (the moral actions of individuals and communities) can we expect pastoral sociology and its critical evaluation to bear the unmistakable marks of vigilance and openmindedness for God's voice as expressed in the voice of our time. Such complete openmindedness will dispose Christians to listen attentively and conscientiously to all the findings of research in order that they may perceive this voice more fully.

The Pastoral Plan with a Socio-Pastoral Basis and the KAIROS

The biblical notion of *kairos* forbids all autonomous and inflexible stereotyped planning that could deter man from a constant vigilance for the needs of the present hour. Therefore, pastoral sociology would render poor service, indeed, to pastoral theology if it were to plan long-range inflexible programs that would not allow for individual initiative and necessary modifications to meet the present need. Such plans are contrary to both the sociological viewpoint and the historic-salvific perspective inherent in the biblical *kairos*. All action modifies reality. In view of human freedom, new unforeseen forces enter constantly into the sociological picture.

Pastoral sociology has much to offer to our time, particularly in evangelization and in pastoral applications to contemporary issues. It is in the application and modification of these principles that ministers and theologians as well as the laity will benefit in their involvement in the secular city. Thus, empirical sociology may contribute much to practical research in the realistic appraisal of the changing situation. This will require a spirit of solidarity and collaboration in both the interpretation and application of socio-pastoral research. In addition, we need to exert a constant vigilance in order to correlate the findings of research with new perspectives arising from the intellectual climate of twentieth-century civilization. This openness to the new dimensions of human existence in the present epoch must guide both clergy and laity. This realistic approach will safeguard the ability for adaptation in due consideration of the eternal laws and the demands of time, in fidelity to duties common to all men and those imposed by the historic moment.

Bibliography

Burkill, T. Alec. "St. Mark's Philosophy of History," *New Testament Studies*. 1956–1957 (Cambridge University Press), 142–48.

Casserley, Julian Victor Longmead. *Toward a Theology of History*. New York: Holt, Rinehart and Winston, Inc., 1965.

Clement, Olivier. *Transfigurer le Temps. Notes on Time in the Light of Orthodox Tradition* (Collection Communauté de Taizé) Paris, 1959.

Conzelmann, Hans "Gegenwart und Zukunft in der synoptischen Tradition," *Zeitschrift für Theologie und Kirche*, LIV (1957), 277–96.

Ibid. The Theology of St. Luke. Translated by Geoffrey Buswell. New York: Harper & Row, 1960.

Cullmann, Oscar. *Christ and Time: The Primitive Christian Conception of Time and History*. Translated from the German by Floyd Filson. Philadelphia: Westminster Press, 1950.

Danielou, Jean. *The Lord of History: Reflections on the Inner Meaning of History*. Translated from the French by Nigel Abercombie. Chicago: Henry Regnery Co., 1958; London: Longmans Green, 1958.

Fromm, Erich. *The Art of Loving*. New York: Harper and Row, 1962.

George, Augustin. "L'heure" de Jean XVII, in *Revue Biblique* LXI (1954), 392–97.

Häcker, Theodor. *Der Christ und die Geschichte*. Leipzig: J. Hegner, 1935.

Löwith, Karl. *Meaning of History; The Theological Implica-*

tions of the Philosophy of History. Chicago: University of Chicago Press, 1949.

Ibid. Nature, History, and Existentialism, and other Essays in the Philosophy of History. Evanston, Ill.: Northwestern University Press, 1966.

Rahner, Karl. "Theologische Prinzipien der Hermenautik eschatologischer Aussagen" *Zeitschrift für katholische Theologie.* (Herder Verlag Wien) LXXXII (1960), 137-58.

Tillich, Paul. *Protestant Era.* Chicago: University of Chicago Press, 1948.

Ibid. The Interpretation of History. New York: Charles Scribner's Sons, 1936.

Index

Index

Index